Heart

Heart
Habib Noorbhai, PhD

Copyright © 2017 Habib Noorbhai, PhD

First edition 2017

All rights reserved. No part of this book may be reproduced or transmitted in any form or by any means, electronic or mechanical, including photocopying, recording or any information storage or retrieval system without permission from the copyright holder.

The Author has made every effort to trace and acknowledge sources/resources/individuals. In the event that any images/information have been incorrectly attributed or credited, the Author will be pleased to rectify these omissions at the earliest opportunity.

ISBN 978-0-620-77939-5

Published by the Author using Reach Publishers' services,
P O Box 1384, Wandsbeck, South Africa, 3631

Edited by Rendale Snow for Reach Publishers
Website: www.reachpublishers.co.za
E-mail: reach@webstorm.co.za

Cover designed by Russell Woolmer

Photographer for cover by David Sharp

Dedicated to those who give and will give, from the heart.

Table of Contents

About the Author		i
Foreword		iii
Synopsis		ix
Prologue		xi

Part 1   **The Inferior Vena Cava**

1. Birth is Not Just an Entrance to the World — 1
2. What Is Beauty And Happiness? — 7
3. Relationships – My Greatest Accomplishment — 16
4. Individuality – "I Am Who I Am" — 21
5. Character is the Basis of All Actions — 26
6. Adapting to Environments — 29
7. Why Intelligence Doesn't Make You Successful — 34
8. The Enemy — 41

Part 2   **The Superior Vena Cava**

9. Education — 49
10. The Move to Cape Town — 68
11. My Perspectives on Leadership — 74
12. Heart — 97
13. The Humanitarians — 111
14. Mr South Africa — 125

Part 3   **The Aorta**

15. Life Stamina — 159
16. Life as a Test — 167
17. The Ultimatum — 171

Acknowledgements	179
Glossary	181

About the Author

Dr Habib Noorbhai (Mr South Africa 2017) is a researcher in Sports Science. He is also a humanitarian, presenter and speaker. He completed a BA in Sport Psychology (UJ), Honours in Biokinetics (UKZN), MPhil in Biokinetics (UCT) and a Ph.D. in Exercise Science at UCT.

Habib has had the pleasure of working with international sports teams (Yorkshire CCC {2012}, South Australian Redbacks cricket team {2010}) and volunteered as an expert on the Health24 website (2012 - 2017).

In 2013, he was among South Africa's 100 brightest young minds and in 2015, he was nominated among *Mail and Guardians* top 200 young South Africans.

Habib also founded an NPO in 2013 called The Humanitarians, a volunteer-based organisation, whereby various community projects and programmes are conducted through sport, health, education, sustainability and innovation. These programmes are also conducted through Habib's current reign as Mr South Africa to spearhead change and to make a difference in society. Recently, he was also included in Fast Company South Africa's Top 30 creative people in business.

Habib has been featured on a variety of television shows, both as a professional and as Mr South Africa. Some of these included *Top Billing*, *Mela*, thrice on *Expresso*, eNCA and SABC News. In 2015, he had his own sport and health show on OpenView HD and a radio show on Hashtag Radio. He is also a frequent guest expert on Cape Talk and 702 radio stations discussing relevant topics on sports science, exercise and health.

Through his memoir, *Heart*, he hopes to inspire as many people as possible to live better lives with a foundation of having a heart. Through the book, he communicates the art of living through humanitarianism, working smart, loving, having a balance and knowing your purpose.

Foreword

Prof. Tim Noakes OMS
MBChB, MD, DSc, Ph.D. (hc), FACSM, (hon) FFSEM (UK), (hon) FFSEM (Ire)
Emeritus Professor of Exercise and Sports Science

It is with the greatest pleasure that I contribute this foreword for this book for one of my most favourite people, Dr Habib Noorbhai. As Habib describes in this book, I came to know the man when he chose me to guide him in his Ph.D. study of the optimum back-lift technique for use by cricket batsmen. I use the word "guide" advisedly because Habib has some unusual abilities that are extremely uncommon even in the very best Ph.D. students. I may have been the "guide" for Habib's thesis but the work is all his own – completed in a manner at which I continue to marvel. Indeed, the story of how he came to choose this unusual topic for his Ph.D. thesis begins to explain the man's defining characteristics.

Since about 2000 I had been interested in an idea, conceived by an Englishman Frank Shillinglaw, that the matchless performances of the greatest cricket batsman of all time, Australian Sir Donald Bradman, were due to his unusual, indeed "unorthodox" batting technique. Shillinglaw has spent the best part of his 30 years tirelessly promoting this idea to all in the cricketing world. Essentially to no avail; no one it seems would take him seriously. Until it turns out, very recently – and at least in part because of the academic attention that Habib has brought to this topic through his Ph.D. research.

You have to ask: If an idea has been around for 30 years yet no one bothers to take it seriously, what will it take to change that attitude? The answer, as always, is that it takes the daring of a single individual who sees the future and wants to cause it to happen. Also, someone who is not scared to ask the difficult questions and to risk the censure of those lesser mortals who live in fear of change and the liberating consequences of discovering new knowledge. I have lived long enough now to understand that such persons are rare and rapidly becoming an endangered species, not just in South African medical science, but also around the world.

So, of the thousands of people with a passion for cricket and the opportunity to study the question, Habib was the only one in the entire world with the courage actually to do something about it. This tells me that he has to be a very unusual citizen. The more I have known him, the more I have begun to appreciate that Habib really is one of those rare and unique individuals that one is truly privileged to meet in the course of one's working life.

Perhaps his most interesting ability is his capacity to complete an enormous amount of work efficiently, in a short space of time and with a minimum of fuss. I learned early on that the best way to assist Habib was to give him a free reign to do what he had already decided and then to help him analyse what his data found.

His ability to complete research tasks is, in my experience, unmatched. I think of the month he travelled around South Africa filming the batting techniques of almost all of South Africa's professional provincial cricketers. Then by filming a large sample of English professional county cricketers, he repeated the same in the United Kingdom, also with a maximum of efficiency and a minimum of fuss.

The result was that within another month he had analysed all the data and produced another chapter for his Ph.D. thesis.

I learned that once Habib decides to do something it would happen regardless of how unlikely I might initially have considered it to be. How possibly could he travel to all these places and be granted permission to film all these players? Simply impossible. "Trust Habib to get it done," however, is a phrase I found myself repeating very often over the past three years.

His only "failure" (in quotation marks) in his ambitions was his inability to organise AB de Villiers and Chris Gayle to be tested in the cricket testing laboratory at the Sri Ramachandra University in Chennai, India. He worked on it for more than a year but in the end, I think it failed to materialise only because of the time constraints imposed on these world's best cricketers.

Besides this extraordinary ability to undertake so much work – in the end, I decided that Habib must sleep only about four hours a night – other characteristics that I appreciated are his ability to be fearless – he is not daunted by any task he sets himself – and his desire to push the boundaries of knowledge, regardless of the personal consequences. He reminds me of another Capetonian, Chris Bertish, the first man to paddle across the Atlantic on a stand-up paddleboard, who teaches that if you can imagine it, you can do it.

I learned too of Habib's very deep knowledge of cricket – as both a player and coach and now as a cricket scientist. For the first time in this book, I discover that Habib had to make the choice between a career in cricket or in academics. Typically, he chose the more difficult initial route – that of being an academic who would have to find the money to put himself through university. Perhaps it would have been easier to seek the security of a salary once he matriculated.

He saw beyond the immediate future.

Another key characteristic is his desire for continuous self-improvement.

Perhaps the most striking example I noticed was when he submitted the first draft of his Ph.D. thesis. On the basis of my and other comments, he decided – it was never suggested by any of us – that he needed some help in upskilling his writing ability. Instead of being affronted by this suggestion (not an uncommon response for almost all of us; how can you possibly suggest that what I write is not already word perfect?), literally within two days, he had discovered that a week-long science writing course would be possible in Durban the following week, so off he went.

The result was that within less than a week he had identified an area he needed to work on; he had found help in another part of the country and had attended the appropriate teaching course, and had enlisted the help of the person running the course. I have not ever experienced this combination of personal abilities and drive in any other student.

His key is the lack of ego and of being open to any help that will advance his desire to be the best possible Habib Noorbhai that he can be, regardless of the criticisms that this drive will inevitably attract from those who lack his courage. Through personal experience, he knows that the path he has chosen will not be welcomed by all, but he has the courage to proceed because his character and his upbringing allow him no other alternative.

When he had completed his thesis he had stepped onto the first rung of the ladder leading towards brilliance – seeing what others have seen but thinking what (almost) no one else has thought and then doing what no one else has done – developing a hypothesis and then collecting data to test that hypothesis. That is the way science advances and through his science, Habib has now made a seminal contribution to our knowledge of the factors determining excellence in cricket batting.

But that is not all. At the same time that he was learning all these skills and desperately wanting to complete his Ph.D. thesis in time for a possible graduation in December 2016, Habib decided that this would not be enough. On top of all this, he entered the Mr South Africa competition, determined to stamp his own personality on that competition.

In particular, Habib wanted to be the first non-professional male model to win the title. He also wanted to change the nature of the competition from narcissism and personal gain (and appearing in a bathing costume) to doing something positive for South Africa.

So his goal was to use the title to undertake humanitarian actions to help under-privileged South Africans. Over the past year, I have marvelled at the extent of the humanitarian actions that he has undertaken – all driven and funded by himself and his unbelievable work ethic.

For as I expected would happen, Habib won the title and has spent 2017 doing exactly as he promised – changing the nature of the responsibilities of the winner of the title. The Mr South Africa competition will never be the same again. Showing that one man determined to do good, can produce change. Even more remarkable is that Habib is principally an academic – what possible knowledge and expertise could he have had in mounting a campaign successfully to win the Mr South Africa competition against many other even more eager competitors?

This book then describes Habib's journey beginning with his roots in a tough environment in which money was not always plentiful but where there was always one abiding, unvarying blessing – the support of a devout family that loves unconditionally. He describes how he is remembered in Johannesburg as "the walker" since for all the years of his tertiary education, his own legs were the only form of transport he could afford. There are not too many of us who have enjoyed that privilege; a privilege that probably more than any other focused Habib's mind on what he wished to do with his mortal life.

This is an inspiring work written by a young man who, despite his absence of years, has already shown that he has so much to offer. He is a story of success against the odds; a testimony that deep conviction and personal endeavour can never be resisted. It is also a story showing that one does not have to be old to make an impact.

My abiding conclusion is that with young people like Habib Noorbhai, the future of South Africa is in good hands. This book helps to explain why.

Synopsis

From birth to death, we are all provided with the same platform to evoke a sustainable and innovative difference in the lives of others, but each and every one of us has a different path or journey. There are a number of factors that contribute towards a person's uniqueness and individuality: the environment, your upbringing and the root. We all have a root within us. The stronger it is, the stronger it will grow. We can grow in maturity, success, value, personal development or within a community.

My root is different.

The book will be structured in three parts:

- **Part 1: The Inferior Vena Cava.** This details the root to my life, mostly written in a philosophical manner;
- **Part 2: The Superior Vena Cava.** This could be described as the meat of my life and career, mostly written in a self-reflective manner;
- **Part 3: The Aorta (closing and way forward).** This is written in both a philosophical and self-reflective manner. The prologue chapter provides an outline and summary of what is covered in the book.

This masterpiece aims to share and inspire people through my life journey prior to, and after Mr South Africa. It showcases the important lessons that I have learnt, together with the fundamental experiences gained as well as the challenges and hard yards that I have faced. At the age of 29, this is not an autobiography. Rather, it is a foundation of what more is to come. Therefore, my foundation is called *Heart*.

When crowned as Mr South Africa, I was also crowned as Mr Heart, because of all the charity projects and initiatives conducted as a contestant. During my reign as Mr South Africa 2017, I embarked on a campaign called 365 days of Heart, where I conducted various types of charity work, outreach or social media posts to inspire and provide aspiration to the youth and society. The book includes #365heart themes as footnotes on each page. I aim to provide quality reading material that readers can assimilate to and understand. Readers can also use the book as a diary to conduct acts of heart or random acts of kindness while reading updated stories of my life (1988 - 2017). At the back of the book, there will be a glossary of 365 days of heart themes with checkboxes, where readers can then tick off which theme they have completed.

We can never be certain of what the future holds but I am certain that my root and the first two branches of life has provided me with a solid foundation to do more for society. After being crowned as Mr South Africa, I remain humbled and grounded; I can never forget where I came from, the hard yards walked and where I am now.

I look to the future now with a better vision and a mission that I hope will make a difference in the lives of others. If I can contribute towards five percent of difference-making, then for me, that would be a significant contribution, and I continue aiming to give from the heart.

I am just an ordinary guy attempting to do extraordinary things – with a foundation of heart.

Prologue

The Root
My family (1988 - 1994)

I can still remember the taste of bread and sardines for dinner – sprinkled, of course, with salt and freshly ground pepper. All the fishy oils sank into the bread. It was a poor man's recipe, but now I realise that it was all part of a grand master plan to shape my character.

I believe that hardship was designed to make you stronger, while easy was designed to make you weaker. My parents weren't well off, but, as with most other parents, there was unconditional love, patience and support in abundance.

Money can't buy that.

It's priceless.

It was never an easy root growing up. When it rained, it poured. When the sun came out, it beamed, in the dry and rat-racing Johannesburg. Our meals were mostly cheap and easy, and often we used candles at night so that we could see each other. I still have some of the bus coupons collected over the years.

A weaker root will find it difficult to wither the storm that I endured, but a stronger root will stand its ground in a variety of unfavourable conditions. I couldn't have asked for a better root.

My root for my love of community goes back a long way.

It started in high school.

Day 1: Live with Purpose #LifePurpose
Day 2: Praise the work of others #WorkOfOthers

I will therefore forever be indebted to my mom, dad, sister and brother for teaching me imperative values and morals. More so, they have given me a conscience for discipline and productivity. This has shaped me in being the driven and passionate man that I am today.

The Bark
Schooling (1995 - 2007)

To be schooled in Johannesburg can be a bit enduring, especially in the area I grew up in. I was mugged, beaten up and a few friends of mine had died in front of me. Not many know this part. I prefer it that way because many things are best to leave in the past, and I prefer to this day not to elaborate on it.

We have so much to be grateful for, and I have always counted my blessings.

I was also bullied for being the quiet type; hard-working and respectable. This had dented a stem in me, but I grew out of it again. Going to school was either by foot, bus or catching lifts with friends. After school, I made my lunch and went back out again for *madressah* (Islamic school) or other extracurricular activities, particularly cricket. In my high school years, we were always part of activities such as market days and clothes and food hamper collections for the needy.

My passion for community work became apparent in my later high school years. It was enjoyable, and it gave me a sense of belonging. Going back home was always great, but on some days it was quiet and lonely. Later on, my sister and brother relocated for work purposes and I missed them a lot. We stayed in front of a park and quite often after going to the mosque, I used to find a quiet space in the park to breathe, walk, think or play sport with members from the neighbourhood.

The First Branch
Undergraduate years (2008 - 2010)

Today, I'm a qualified biokineticist, but growing up I actually dreamt of becoming a cricketer. In fact, I had to choose between county cricket in the United Kingdom or studying towards a Bachelor's in Sport Psychology from the University of Johannesburg (UJ).

This was one of the biggest turning points in my life. I had just completed matric, and I was faced with a daunting choice. Most boys would've opted to become the next Don Bradman or Sachin Tendulkar, but I don't regret choosing UJ instead of the UK.

I received a small bursary from UJ to play cricket for them.

To this day, many people in Jozi (Johannesburg) remember me as "the walker". Each day, I walked from home to university which took me about 45 minutes. I vividly remember that one enduring road along the way, Mercury Road in the suburb of Crosby.

It was so good for my fitness because of the uphill walk, but I always looked forward to coming back home because it was a downhill.

On Tuesdays to Thursdays it was cricket practice, so I had to walk with my "coffin" (cricket bag). It was heavy, but it was my form of training, carrying the bag alternating between each shoulder. I walked the university mile every day for two years. I had no choice. Perhaps it wasn't the greatest idea, though. I re-injured my lower back severely and couldn't play cricket for another six months.

My first back injury was in matric (2007) – an injury that shattered my dream of becoming a professional cricketer. If I were a biokineticist then and knew better, I would have tried an alternative plan. Needless to say, my bursary in my second and third year fell through.

I continued, however, with my role as cricket coach at Parkview Senior School. This was another uphill battle. From UJ to Parkview was at least a 90-minute walk. At least I had legs to die for, although I dreaded it, especially on Tuesdays and Thursdays.

It meant a total of 270 minutes of walking per day. That is 135 minutes going and 135 minutes coming back. I simply couldn't afford to take a bus or a taxi. I was earning a mere R150 a day and coached cricket two days a week.

In a month, I was getting roughly between R1,050 and R1,200. That was enough for my meals, airtime and the odd coffee with friends. My parents were working-class people and could only afford the bare essentials at home. I am grateful that they taught me gratitude, appreciation and did not spoil me, but a plan had to be made for my university fees.

I was always the daredevil type of guy who wanted to try my hand at most things. I learnt the concept of cricket coaching clinics when I saw something on TV one day. I then started having cricket coaching clinics every holiday for children around Johannesburg. It was called the HN Cricket Coaching Academy. Little did I know that many years later I would still be using my "HN brand", named after my initials.

Sure, the academy was a means of earning bucks and paying for all those little items that I so desperately needed, but it became so enjoyable. Cricket coaching increased my love for children. At one point I conducted a clinic with no profit. I didn't mind because I enjoyed working with the boys and helping them improve their game.

Day 7: We should always be grateful for fresh water #FreshWater
Day 8: A person of honour doesn't hesitate to take the lead #Lead

But I couldn't be profitless for every clinic. I eventually made some profit and paid for my fees in my second and third year at UJ. Mr. Feizal Kimmie, a cricket enthusiast and mentor, played an imperative role during these years and I will never forget him and his wife, Zara.

"When you work hard to get somewhere, you will need to work even harder to stay there," had always been my motivation. Just like cricket, we work for every 10 runs scored and the last ten runs of a 100 is usually the hardest.

I wanted to become a biokineticist to help athletes with their rehabilitation because I knew what it took after being injured. Knowing how it felt and studying it, was, however, two different things. Out of a pool of approximately 100 undergraduate students, universities were only accepting between 10 and 15 Honours students.

The selections were tough.

I persevered, made the requirements and got accepted into the University of Johannesburg, the University of Western Cape, University of Witwatersrand, as well as the University of KwaZulu-Natal (UKZN) to continue my Honours studies. Until today, I tell myself that I should have stayed at UJ for my Honours because I would have been a better biokineticist. At the time I was informed that they emphasised a lot more on practical experience than research aspects.

I don't regret it though. Otherwise, I wouldn't have had a passion for research. UKZN had ignited my passion for research, and it was my choice of university to study Honours. Why? I missed my brother a lot and wanted to spend time with him. I was also tired of Johannesburg and wanted a change of scenery. I eventually moved to Durban in 2011 where I completed my Honours.

Day 9: *Take a load off of someone; it might motivate that person to keep going #LoadOff*
Day 10: *Appreciate the talents in others and encourage them to move forward #Talents*

The second branch
Post-graduate years (2012 - 2016)

As a Jozi boy who had now tasted the Durban life, I always wondered what it would be like to live in the Mother City. I heard it was beautiful, and as a biokineticist, I had my eye on the Sports Science Institute of South Africa (SSISA).

The SSISA had a reputation for being an incredible place to work at. I was mildly intrigued. In 2009, one of our second-year lecturers referred to it as the "Lore of Running" for our Exercise Physiology lecture.

The lecturer encouraged us to meet the well-known scientist, Professor Tim Noakes if we ever had the opportunity – even if it was once in our lifetimes as he is a remarkable man. In 2011, in my Honours year, we were lectured on sports injury rehabilitation, and our lecturer then said something similar about Tim. I then knew that it was my calling. I had to make my way to Cape Town and work with him but always knew that it would be difficult as he was very sought after and had many students that he supervised.

I eventually got accepted as an intern at SSISA as well as the University of Cape Town's (UCT) Masters in Biokinetics programme. Moving to Cape Town was the best decision that I could have made. When I moved there, however, I knew no one.

I then understood why I was alone most of the time growing up. It was times like these that my earlier years prepared me for. I moved into UCT's Obz Square residence. I have so many fond memories of the relationships formed there between 2012 and 2014. Although our rooms were only 11 square metres, it had uncapped Wi-Fi and free laundry services on the ground floor.

My dream of working with Tim became a reality in 2014.

Day 11: Poor health affects performance; show your support #SupportHealth
Day 12: *A healthy body leads to a healthy mind #Healthy*

After I completed my MPhil, I registered for a Ph.D. in Exercise Science at UCT doing a thesis on one of my passions – the rather bizarre research subject of cricket batting. Tim was my supervisor not just throughout my Ph.D., but it was also his mentorship, inspiration, humility and character that showed me what a remarkable man he is.

When I meet with Tim, he always teaches and inspires me, and I'm often reminded of a similar distinguished personality, the late Former President Nelson Mandela, my role-model. The works of Madiba accentuated my passion and drive to do more for communities and society.

When I came to Cape Town, I found it challenging to do community work compared to Jozi and Durban. I also got used to the laid-backness of the city, and after a few months, I couldn't wait any longer. I then decided to start my own heart-driven emporium called The Humanitarians. The last six years in Cape Town has been a journey of character and professional development.

The third branch
(2017>)

We can never be quite certain of what the future holds, but I am confident that my root and first two branches of life have provided me with a solid foundation to do more. After being crowned as Mr South Africa in 2016, I remain humbled and grounded.

I can never forget where I came from, the hard yards walked and where I am now.

Sure, I can say a lot more about what transpired in my earlier years, but I tried to be as concise as possible and rather speak about the main lessons and turning points. Additional insights,

---

Day 13: Variety is the spice of life; let's shake it up #Variety
Day 14: Love comes in many forms, show you care #Love

experiences and lessons will be provided later on in the book.

I certainly believe that what I have achieved so far stems from the hardships and obstacles that I have encountered and experienced growing up. My life calling is to educate, inspire and make a difference through research, humanitarianism and the media.

I salute and thank all the "leaves" that played an integral part of my first and second branches. I look forward to meeting more leaves and hope that the life I live will be a tree of abundance, inspiration and in service to others.

Your life is a message to the world.

Make sure it's inspiring and leave a legacy behind.

Laugh, live, love and make a difference.

Day 15: *Talk is cheap; we must do more #DoMore*

Day 16: *Beauty is hidden in the detail; find it today and appreciate the little findings #Beauty*

PART 1
THE INFERIOR VENA CAVA

1
Birth is Not Just an Entrance to the World

We all enter this world innocent and helpless, screaming our lungs out for that gasp of air to redeem our right to this rollercoaster of a journey called life. Whether it is life as a human or from a hatching chicken egg, life in itself is precious and is a blessing. Life as we know it and what we come to know, is not what it all seems to be.

Plans will never work out, and the unexpected will happen. Such is the miracle of birth and its endeavours. For some it is unexpected, but for others, it is planned. It is the one situation that can be planned, but it too doesn't come at an easy pace. When it's planned, it is seen as the greatest blessing that can ever happen in the lives of most parents and their families.

Just like a seed planted in the soil that grows up to be a plant, we were once all just a seed, a zygote to be exact. Once conception took place, we grew inside God's greatest gift to man, a mother's womb, for nine long months. Even though some are eager to enter this world earlier than their due date, those months are what creates the bond between what some of us are lucky enough to call our mother today.

A plant can be used in the same essence to describe life as a human being. Plants grow from seedlings into beautiful flowers or

---

Day 17: Know your calling and share it with others #Calling
Day 18: Do an activity that leads from the heart #HeartfulAct

perhaps a big willow tree. They also start off small and innocent and express their need to be alive through the action and phase of growth. We are all part of the big willow tree of life in that we are all leaves on this tree. Each leaf will weather with whatever the storm may bring.

Changes may occur to these leaves through the different seasons. Some may fall off or inhabit another tree. Just like the leaves on the tree of life, we shall all change in time and survive, and some will eventually leave the tree to seek other avenues.

We, as humans, may leave this world as the leaves shall through degradation, both to the same resting place, the soil. The choices for plants and trees are endless and so too is life for us.

We may start off small and helpless, but with the possibilities out there, we reach higher statuses and end up, if we are lucky enough, to be more in control of our lives with the decisions we make. However, we later realise that we are only in control of the decisions and not our fate. Roads may diverge, but we will end up at our destiny.

That seems to be the aim of most human beings but as you will find reading through this book, the meaning of life is different to each one of us, but it could be the same if we all have some guidance towards the fact that we all have a purpose in life. If we can focus on that purpose, then our lives will be fulfilled. To get to that purpose, our mindsets need to be correct, and that starts from childhood and what and who we are exposed to, all impact on the lives we lead. However, it all starts from the heart before it even goes to the point of being a concept of mindset, but we will speak about heart later.

Some will be lucky enough to have discovered their purpose whereas others will search their whole lives for it and still won't find it when they pass on. Let us have a look at the beginning of life and how we could gear our children towards seeing this purpose even from such a young age.

As a child, our actions can be somewhat limited. Most children eat, sleep, babble and poop. Simple. That is the daily routine in which most parents are personal assistants to their children. The only freedom some children have is to the end of their cots and back or rocking back and forth in their high chairs.

As babies we get fed by our parents, told when to sleep and though we may not control our bowels at this age, our guardians control where we carry out this deed. Our parents or guardians protect us from the evil world which we shall experience later on in life, but for now, we are shielded.

Our parents veil us from the world and its evil wishing to keep us small and innocent in efforts to protect us as they know how cruel the world out there is. If this were ideal, then we would not be able to find our meanings in life and follow our hearts towards our dreams and tribulations.

For me, it was not always an easy root growing up.

When it rained, it poured. When the sun came out, it beamed, in the dry and rat-racing Johannesburg. I remember the taste of bread and sardines for dinner, the use of candles at night so that we could see each other and the number of bus coupons kept over the years. Hardship is designed to make you stronger and easy is designed to make you weaker. A weaker root will find it difficult to weather the storm, but a stronger root will stand its ground in a variety of unfavourable conditions. I couldn't ask for a better root! It has shaped me towards writing this memoir, *Heart*.

Ironically, I had developed a murmur of the heart when I was little. I subsequently developed asthma and had difficulty breathing, especially when playing sports. This was known as exercise-induced

---

Day 21: Bullying is not tolerated in striving for a better country #Anti-bullying
Day 22: Practise gratitude, as this keeps one grounded #Gratitude

asthma. I had to use a pump daily as prescribed by the doctor. That was until one day, playing football and learning how to swim did the trick.

I was weaned off the pump, and the essence of having a murmur of the heart did not affect me. The other reason why the irony of life is also beautiful is that I was also crowned as Mr Heart South Africa last year, for all the charity projects and initiatives I conducted as a contestant leading up to the final. Also, my mom constantly laughs with joy and pride, at the fact that her son who had a murmur of the heart and who didn't like to be active, is a biokineticist and sport scientist today?

From birth, we try our best, but we also trust in God's plan for us.

Furthermore, we are all born with the blueprint for language, the means by which we communicate. We all have the universal means of language, but how we utilise it and the different languages we speak, can influence our way of life. There are many ways in which we can make our lives different, and that is through the choices we make that is surrounded by our intellectual, spiritual and physical being.

At the stage proceeding birth, our spiritual and physical being is limited by our guardians, but it is our intellectual capabilities that govern the early stages of the life path we shall take. Being more intellectually inclined during this stage is an advantage in that it shows one would excel faster than others and perhaps choose a career path with the various characteristics in that regard. Essentially, as we know, up to the first six years of life is the foundation and development of a human being. The need for every bit of stimulation; physical, intellectual or cognitive, is imperative.

To highlight the importance of the above point, each moment during our childhood is essential to moulding us into who we are later in life. The importance of bedtime stories and exposure to

---

Day 23: Success lies on the other side of fear #Success
Day 24: *Have a vision for your country and make it your mission #VisionAndMission*

reading has a great impact on a child's ability to cope with the literacy demands when he or she enters school. It is important for every parent to provide to the best of their ability the best childhood upbringing they can.

The repercussions of this are seen later in children's lives and during their schooling career where they battle to cope. All this could have a cascade effect leading to low self-esteem, being bullied, extra tuition involved and leads to where our children end up not achieving their goals and perhaps being unsatisfied, miserable or reaching a state of stagnancy within their lives.

As children, we are what can be described as present hedonist beings. It may sound a bit evil, but it simply means that we worry less about pain and more about pleasure at this stage of our lives. We are shielded and limited by our parents in our environments. We live for the day as at this stage we are living off our parent's expectations and orders. We are given the freedom to imagine if we are fortunate enough to be exposed to the wonderful world of reading but that is where the line is drawn.

We are not encouraged at this stage to dream of our future or our career paths. The future, therefore, is not on our mind; rather it is a time of innocent fun and play without considering any or minimal consequences. It would be healthier for parents to expose their children to difficult situations that require their parents' assistance. This will help the children to familiarise and fend for themselves should they be in those compromising situations later on in life.

As we move on to our teenage years, when we begin to resource ourselves, (just like plants grow by essential resources and as one will read in this book) we rebel if we do not agree with the strong dominance from our guardians – the trademark of a teenager – as we are still finding our way, our purpose. In this regard, we can see

---

Day 25: Show kindness to animals, they too need our love and support #Animals
Day 26: Capture a moment that will last a lifetime #CaptureMoments

that we start developing a somewhat minor control in our lives.

As famously narrated in *The Alchemist* by Paul Coelho, 'there's a path for all of us'. When we are young, we are fearless and not afraid to dream. There are forces that will appear negative, but actually, they help us realise the dream even more. We are taught to marvel the world, but it would help if we were taught or even made aware of the drops of oil on the spoon.

Birth in itself is so fascinating, and I believe it is the best gift to humanity from God. The fact that a woman has been given this miracle called a womb to grow her seeds highlights the importance of women from that aspect. We may start off innocent but once we grow up, life can influence us, and we can take on any shape as mentioned.

As we grow up learning from our environment, we soon become a person that is unique. Yes, our genetic make-up makes us physically unique, but it is the aspects that we now have control over such as our spiritual being that enables us to be who we want to be.

If we go back to the picture of our willow tree and flowering plants, the growth of that plant during the different storms and interaction with the environment, shapes the plant to produce flowers, offspring or take a different path of no flowers and it may just wither away. As we can see, life is just like the growth of a plant, and our individuality is one such characteristic in conjunction with our environment that stems from our mental uniqueness. Birth is the start of life, and there are many influences and attributes to it.

In any way, God gives us this gift.
Love them unconditionally.
Birth is precious. Birth is beautiful. It is the root of life.
Where there is a root, there is life.
Birth is not just an entrance to the world.

2
What Is Beauty And Happiness?

Eyes are the best weapon.

It is the word beauty that creates the most controversy and disease in life.

It is the word – beauty – that changes a person's life.

What is beauty?

Who is beauty?

Where is it found?

We all have our interpretation, and I will share mine. Beauty is something that we can see, we can hear, we can touch and think. It is universal. It is everywhere. We overlook and undermine it every day. You and I, we are all unique and beautiful in our way. The combination of our elements makes us who we are. We are beautiful but because we have symbols of beauty and what we should look like, our image is distorted, and that is where disease, unhappiness and depression, and even suicide comes in. We could answer these questions stated above simply.

Behind those eyes lie amazing and unimaginable experiences towards your life.

Beauty does not define who we are. Our characteristics don't either, the intention does, and actions do. This is linked to beauty, inner beauty.

Day 29: Never give up on your dreams, start making it a reality #Dream
Day 30: Giving people hope is the most powerful tool you can give #Hope

We get old – we lose our appearance, people get burnt, people get diseases. When they lose their physical appearance and beauty, then what? We leave that person because they no longer appeal to us? Yes, we need physical attraction, but it's the heart that captures us eventually. It sounds strange, but it does happen. Those people go for what we call materialism. This leaves us with the question: What do you go for? The golden apple or just an apple?

The concept of hearing what we deserve – we hear it all the time. You deserve someone beautiful? Yes, from the heart or physically? If you don't know; then your priorities are all wrong. You could choose both and wouldn't even know it. Usually, the outside does not match the inside. The inside remains forever but not the outside; unless you are blessed with amazing genes. Regardless though, beauty is in the eyes of the beholder.

Behind those eyes, those hard yards walked, is the body with the heart and hands, doing good things, teaching it to others, helping others – like my mother. The true self lies in that which we never see in the people we come across on the street. So take the time to greet, smile at and get to know someone who interests you.

Go on blind dates. I have been on one before, but I'll speak about relationships later. You will surprise yourself and others. Behind those eyes lie hurt and sorrow as well. Eyes can often be used in accordance with body language, to tell a person's mood, as well as other techniques which should be a good reductionist.

Some search for economic wealth thinking that it brings happiness. These aspects are all related to happiness and intertwined. Some seek materialism, but in the end they find out too late that money doesn't bring happiness nor does it do anything for you but help you to survive. Why should we worry about this big house and that fancy car?

Day 31: Embracing sustainable giving and moving away from toxic charity is a meaningful change #NoToxicCharity

Day 32: Picking up and recycling litter enhances a green and eco-friendly environment #Litter

Yes, it's a personal achievement, but if your house had to burn down, you would only take your loved ones. That's where the importance lies. We indebt ourselves buying the greatest of everything because others have it; it's the latest must-have trends. These things bring temporary happiness and perhaps instant gratification, but not emotional happiness; that happiness that makes you smile from within. Growing up, most of us didn't have these luxuries and life was so much simpler.

Nowadays children know more than us about iPads, cell phones and various other technologies. Materialism. Our downfall. We never had these things because it was never a necessity. Getting our hands dirty and competing with who could get more plasters on their body was the "in thing". This was the foundation of happiness, keeping it clean, yet real.

Sadly, materialism and greed lead to recession and rules the world where poverty is side-lined; where my heart crumbles. Life, in my opinion, is the success of all, and it is possible. But we don't make it possible – because we simply don't want to.

When we die we go with ourselves in whichever religion we believe or don't believe in. The Egyptians believed in the afterlife and their coffins were lined with gold, and all their wealth was put in with them. Years later, the coffin is still gold, and the items are still there, but the bodies are not. Dawn to dusk; life to dust, and back to life again – resurrecting to the hereafter. A question I keep asking: do I chase the beauty and happiness of this world or the next?

Seeking materialism is a waste of time, money and effort, which can be invested elsewhere such as in your family or truly increasing your happiness and quality of life. Doing for others – that's my calling, it makes me happy. It fills the soul with the sole, and the

---

Day 33: *Paying attention to the homeless helps make a better nation #Homeless*
Day 34: *Help improve someone's day with a precious gift #Gift*

heart with warmth.

Living in a big house may increase your quality of comfort but ultimately, family, love, support and taking care of yourself, increases the quality. It's the simple things that count. Money may help the world go around but eating healthy increases our quality of life; the other things are luxuries. Is it toxic or sustainable?

Think about it.

We can have nothing but if we have good hearts and intentions, and if we believe in God, God gives and provides and He takes away. If you don't believe in God, I have nothing against you, but you may believe in a divine spirit or energy.

Nothing guarantees you anything, but it does improve the quality of your being. Some are blessed on this earth. I am very happy for them, and actually, exceptionally proud. But I believe the blessed should aim for the hereafter. It's not how much they earn, achieve or have. It's what they do with that wealth that counts.

We shouldn't be getting awards for helping out when this is what we as human beings should be doing as our duty; or more mildly – our moral code. That's what humanitarianism or philanthropy does to us – it enhances our moral code. Our hearts are beautiful and will never change metaphorically but physically they will with age. They remain forever; they have a beat for a reason, and the beating frequencies alter for a reason. Physical, outer beauty does not last except in those rare cases without interference cosmetically. We will all grow old, it is inevitable.

Death is inevitable as well – accept it.

Make-up is another story. Why? Tell me why? Yes, it enhances your features but not when one can literally scrape off the make-up. I will never understand why those that don't need the make-up overdo it. I never wear make-up - even for photo shoots or being

---

Day 35: *Embracing women's worth through sustainable dialogue #RespectWomen*
Day 36: *Contribute towards building an active and healthier nation #Exercise*
Day 37: *Motivate students to keep pushing, despite the challenges #Persevere*

on camera, purely because my skin is also sensitive to it. My scars tell a story. It has a history. Why should I hide it? Be authentic. Be real.

How one looks does not define nor carry one's worth. It is something which is very different for all and not important. Yet many behave as though it holds more value than the inside, especially when it comes to choosing spouses. People are degraded when they don't look a certain way: fair skin, green eyes, tall? I hate it!

Who says that physical beauty makes us different from one another? "You sure you want to wake up the next morning sleeping next to one minute past midnight?" Racist, inappropriate and ignorant. My response: "It may be one minute or even 10 minutes past midnight, but if the heart is pure and light, then I wouldn't only want to wake up next to that person but also watch her sleep".

If it's your preference, I respect it but don't degrade that person to the rest of us. Your parents want the best for you, and you deserve this emotionally but not physically. You ultimately know what's good for you, which is what appeals to you and what makes you happy.

Beauty cannot be seen, heard or touched. Beauty can only be felt as it is within the heart. We can't see it as the measure of beauty is not possible. God alone is the sole judge and knows how beautiful you truly are; no award can determine your beauty.

No one can judge you because they don't know what beauty is, or what your journey is. We have society's interpretation, and then we have our own. All these images of what is perfect come back to the question: what is beauty?

We all have opinions. Some may agree with others, but at the end of the day, we will never know. Perfection does not exist. I don't even know why the word was invented. How can we describe

---

Day 38: Provide hope and assistance for persons who need it #Assistance
Day 39: Help give someone a break during work hours #WorkingBreak
Day 40: Breaking poverty is better than fuelling it #BreakPoverty

heaven and hell when we don't even know the truth? The human being is fooled, and we are gullible. It's the beauty of the unknown.

Just like the heart, it is a beautiful yet unknown place. Don't reject the heart because its outer shell has added layers of subcutaneous adipose tissue or a different shade of earth sand. Beauty is in the heart, and no one can tell you if you are beautiful or not. If they do, for whatever their reason is, say: "Thank you. You are just as beautiful because you identified something beautiful in me."

Beauty comes from within, and you will only feel it when you believe that you are beautiful, and unfortunately, that only comes with heartache and time. You can't be something you are not; you can only be you. People have different ideas of beauty, and if you conform to it, you will miss the beauty of yourself.

Materialism is relative. Humility is rare. A good example of this, of those who have it all, was the late Princess Diana, and now Princes William and Harry. They say change if you don't like what you see in the mirror. There is nothing wrong with that, but the problem arises when it takes over our lives, and that is not what life is about. Who are we? We are beautiful in our special way, which no one can touch or see but only marvel at.

This is a new concept brought about by the evolution of man. The luxuries in those days were eating a good meal, while these days it's the house you live in or that fancy car you drive. When you focus on these things, you miss out on life, you truly do. Don't let life pass you by, waking up early to get to a sale of your favourite fashion brand, or even spending a whole day choosing a car. At the end of the day, you leave with nothing in this world. We all get driven in a hearse to the grave. Mind you, the life in the grave is a lot longer, without any worldly pleasures. You just take your good deeds with, nothing else.

Day 41: *One of the channels to improve youth sport participation, is through the parents #YouthSport*

Day 42: *Partake in a simple act of kindness by giving an ear to someone random about how their day is going and make them smile #GiveAnEar*

It is your being and heart that is important, cherish those and beautify them.

Do for others; we are all equal. No one says you cannot reward yourself but there are limits, and that comes when the time could be spent more wisely doing something else. Your life must be productive for the right reasons. The concept of a wedding being so extravagant these days and putting yourself in debt is beyond human understanding. There is nothing wrong with celebrating the day, but celebrate it for the right reasons, most especially for love and families coming together. Instead of having a reception, feed a community with your bride/husband. This is something I want to do one day!

I envision a 10- or 20-person wedding, including the bride, groom, five family members each, and done. Then take all of them with to the community and feed them, sustainably. Try it, and you will have more money and time, less stress and more time to spend with those who matter most. Hey, why not just get married, travel the world and then return to your lives.

Don't even post on social media – it has taken over our beautiful lives! Although each of us will have varied reasons for using it, we must try to use it for the right reasons. Life moments are so precious, and many people don't get the chance to experience them because of stress and work. We only realise when it's too late, 'you only know you love her/him when you let her/him go'. Well, it can be generalised to all situations; for anyone.

Happiness is underrated and overlooked. It is the answer to everything, spiritual and health-wise. If we are happy, then everything is positive in our lives even when things are not great. It is the happiness that keeps us going. Happiness comes in many forms, but the truly special one that gives us long life is the happiness felt from

---

***Day 43**: There is no limit on how much community health one can provide #NoCommunityLimit*

***Day 44**: A non-profit organisation should not just be a round table discussion; it needs to be active and implementable #ImplementableCharity*

love. Love from family and the all-important love from that special one.

I will finish this chapter off with a short story.

Beauty lies in the eyes of skinny jeans.

No, really.

Beauty lies in the eye of the beholder, so they say. We are only human and can only be ourselves, yet we want to be other people. People write about this everywhere and the influence of what beauty is, is overrated. Yes, beauty is in the eye of the beholder, but saying this, doesn't make it any easier to accept it.

For years I was told I was ugly and I believed those who told me this because I measured beauty on others, by their status in the limelight. That popularity told me that they were beautiful, and they always got what they wanted. When I started realising what I wanted, then I saw beauty.

Beauty is in the heart. It is something that is never seen and can never be judged. Beauty on the outside, now that's great, but hey, that's just your genetic makeup. That is what you were entitled to. The essence of your heart, on the other hand, is not part of your genetic makeup, and that I believe, determines the nature of a person. The heart of a person, mind you, is not static and it can change for better or for worse. When it is in the true and sincere position, then beauty shines throughout your whole body regardless of whether your features are complementary or not.

Who am I to judge? Think for yourselves, am I beautiful or just in it for the ride? We all want more than what life gives us, but we fail to realise that we make our lives what they are based on the nature

---

Day 45: *Follow up on a prior act of kindness; monitoring and evaluation is key #MnE*
Day 46: *Don't leave a place untidy, help pack away even if it's not your mess #PackAway*
Day 47: *Show etiquette to waiters and always give them a tip; it is considerate #Waiters*

of our hearts. The outcome is present, but the road we take is of utmost importance.

The road less taken is shunned by others and the courage to rise above also makes us beautiful. What is beauty anyway? Eye colour, if one can fit into those skinny jeans, if you can get any partner you want, if you succeed in life, if you perm your hair a certain way? Who knows! But our hearts have the answer.

Am I beautiful? Maybe, I just have almond shaped eyes that complement my face yet I have a crooked tooth that some would say is unpleasant. The meaning of beauty will always differ from person to person, and we will never know who is beautiful as it lies in that person's heart and in the people that benefit from the person's existence.

Day 48: Educate people on the meaning of a humanitarian #MeaningOfHumanitarian
Day 49: Explain with an illustration what humanitarianism really means #Illustration
Day 50: Show support and care towards the deaf community #DeafCommunity

3
Relationships – My Greatest Accomplishment

A vast majority of people work or are in contact with other people on a daily basis. To me, people are the greatest asset and not things which are wrapped in gold or silver (materialistic items). Money might make the world go round, but people are the ones who drive it. The true essence and meaning of life can only be experienced when you are part of or with another counterpart. This is known as a relationship (professional, personal, family, friendship and so on).

Along with life, friends have come and gone. People's paths have separated either because of career, personal choices or purely because they didn't complement each other. We start to mature when we begin to realise that we must dissociate from those who are toxic and lead us towards toxic environments.

Despite such differences among people, and although every person is unique, we learn to respect and appreciate them for who they are.

For me, my greatest accomplishment in life has been the relationships that I have either fostered, maintained or the ones that I have chosen to dissociate myself from. Although we try our best to be good and authentic to every single person, there is, unfortunately,

---

Day 51: *Give an idea to someone to prevent them from sleeping on an empty stomach #SustainableIdea*
Day 52: *Help a shift worker get through the night #ShiftWorker*

going to be a select few who are just not your cup of tea. Your job is to try and make it work, but your job is not to please them to make it work.

Principles and integrity are everything. Even after forgiveness doesn't work, don't keep a grudge, forgive them within and move on. The poison can either be coughed out or go through the digestive process. Forgiving each other or parting ways amicably is a means of coughing the poison out.

After numerous attempts of trying to make it work or offering an apology and there is still no light at the end of the tunnel, allow the poison to digest (this will take time), remove the grudge and forgive within. Former President Nelson Mandela has taught us that forgiveness removes fear, it alleviates the soul; this is why it is such a powerful weapon.

Relationships have been the greatest accomplishment for me, not because you get something out of them, no (that is secondary). It has been my greatest accomplishment because people begin to accept and love you for who you are.

A smile is the first instinct – the one deed that can either remove a barrier between two people or start a conversation. Through having a good relationship with people, one realises that career, work, studying or personal goals are secondary or tertiary. The mere fact is, you should not be contacting them or being good to them to further your own personal goals.

Forgiveness and not holding grudges against people is a powerful virtue. Another virtue, which I am yet to experience, is true love in another counterpart. Some people will say true love exists with those who have experienced it. My verdict is that when it is too good to be true, it usually is. But I haven't experienced it yet.

To this day, I have not been in a relationship with a woman. The

---

Day 53: It is not knowledge that is dangerous, but the poor use of it #Knowledge
Day 54: Show support towards a novel programme #ProgrammeSupport

reasoning is complex. Through playing cricket in high school and for our local club, I got to meet a girl through her brother who was a friend that I played cricket with (in 2005). At the time, there was something called Mxit (a chat platform and minor version of WhatsApp), but we had to log in to chat to someone or message them to go online so that we could chat.

I will not reveal her name. I will protect it and rather use, 'she'. She and I used to chat on Mxit. This was the first girl I had a connection with, even though I hadn't met her. Weird, right? But we would have conversations on Mxit, usually most days after school. After some months, I asked her out. She said no.

I respected her decision.

We carried on our friendly conversations. After a few months again, I asked her out. This time she said yes. We were 'together' through a long-distance relationship. She was in and out of Dubai because her family had business on that side. Within these two years, we probably had only met three times. I was serious about her. I wanted to marry her straight after school. Her heart was everything to me. I didn't have to be around her – even though I wanted to. But when Noorbhai's fall for someone, they fall hard.

To cut a long story short, it was towards the end of my matric year (2007) and at this stage we rarely chatted. I was busy with matric examination preparations, but other than this, the reason that we had barely chatted was unknown to me. I continuously wondered why; even sending messages of apology in case I had done something wrong.

Her family's shop was at the Oriental Plaza in Johannesburg. I went to visit them to ask if her brother was okay (indirectly asking if she was okay). If they knew about her and me, we both could have been in trouble. My family knew, but they didn't think it would be serious, despite how laughable it seemed at times.

Her uncle was at the shop. I recognised him because I had played cricket with him too. I asked where he (her brother) was. He said he had gone for his sister's wedding. I said, "But his elder sister is already married?"

He said: "No, his younger sister is getting married."

The empty swallow of heartache. Not knowing how to respond, I just said, "Thank you, please give him my regards," and slowly walked away. I had taken a taxi to the shop but it was a slow walk back home (1 hour and 15 minutes in total).

I was in disbelief.

I was betrayed.

Why couldn't she tell me herself? She had an arranged marriage. This is what I was told. Was she scared to tell me? The fact that I heard from someone else was the worst.

To fast forward, I wrote my matriculation exams. I passed with exemption (the marks were not great), and I got into university. While at university, there would be women approaching me, wanting to chat or perhaps exploring the possibility of getting to know me or date me. I said that I was unfortunately not interested. Yes, at this point, a bitter taste was planted in my mouth, I had trust issues. I knew I couldn't have trust issues for too long and prayed that this feeling would go away.

However, I thanked her for putting me in this situation. She allowed me to defer all distractions and just focus on my studies and career. I only really started chatting to women again and was open to meeting them when I moved to Cape Town (the later chapter).

This bitter seed that was planted was a seed of accomplishment. If I had met other women or spent time getting to know them, I don't think I could have reached this far in my career or would have

---

Day 57: Help make sign language an official language in your country #SignLanguage
Day 58: Share a chat and ear with someone who has similar visions and passions for the community #Synergy

been entirely focused. That lesson at the end of school had shaped me, and it made me stronger. I only told a few about it. I had kept my head down, forgave her internally, removed the grudge, learnt the lesson and moved on.

She messaged me on Facebook in 2016. I was surprised. I never expected to hear from her again. We spoke briefly about what had happened, and I came to a space of closure. I had already forgiven her. In fact, I am so happy for her and her husband. She has the most adorable children, and I hope that they will be her eternal joy.

As I write this, I no longer have trust issues. I know that I was in a different, younger space when it happened. Not all women are like that. In fact, I have met beautiful (inside and out) ladies since overcoming my trust issues, either through university, work or through mutual friends. I look forward to meeting my future counterpart. Perhaps I have met and known her already; we can't be too sure.

I end this chapter off by saying that good and bad relationships have been the greatest accomplishment in my life. I learnt from them, I grew from them, and they taught me how to be cautious, tactful and to always wear a smile on my face, despite the situation. To every single person's path of life that I have crossed, there have been elements that I have learnt from you.

Day 59: Support fellow colleagues on their journeys and challenges #Support
Day 60: Give thought to those who are blind and cannot see #TheBlind

4
Individuality – "I Am Who I Am"

We live in a world where the world itself dictates who we should be in all facets of being a human. Society poses "the perfect" being and we, being gullible enough, fall for it and aspire to be "it". The stronger ones can work against this force, but others fail horribly and end up becoming this generic "perfect" being. Not only are they unhappy but their lives become ruined. This is the way life, and most societies, are unfortunately structured.

When we say "perfect" being in all facets, it is referring not only to a physical state but also to intellectual, spiritual and psychological states. It may not affect every facet of your life, but at some point, I promise you, society dictated or will still dictate your existence in this world.

So why can't we be who we are? What is so wrong with that? We fight inner battles with ourselves day in and day out but for what? We should be proud of who and what we are. "For who you are? For what you are?" Confusing questions, right? Think about it. I mean there is no one like us, we are unique and contribute to our individuality, so why be someone else that already exists?

The number one answer to the before mentioned question is acceptance. Number two is fear. Number three, is because it is easy,

---

Day 61: *Order a surprise meal for someone via a food application #Surprise*
Day 62: *Take a friend out for a movie #MovieTreat*

the 'low' road out.

Let's look at the existence of a plant as a reference; a plant's life depending on its environment is also controlled or dictated in a way. In its natural habitat, its competitors, scavengers and predators dictate the plant's life. In an urban area, humans control the plant's life. Likewise, we are also controlled. No two people are the same. We can share some traits but will never have the exact compilation as another person. The probability is too small to even comprehend. Even monozygotic twins are 99,9% identical. The other 0,01% is due to environmental variation. The art of genetics!

As teenagers growing up, we can be stigmatised and bullied. We can't be who we want to be or who we need to be. This makes getting through situations, be they at school, socially, or on the sports field, difficult. What we need to be is what society depicts as 'normal', and that is limiting.

I was bullied for being quiet, hard-working and respectable. This dented a stem in me, but I grew out of it. It happens to this day – bullying, because you bring in an element that is either unique or out of the ordinary. And then you become the boss or mentor of the person who bullied you. The irony of life. Priceless!

The impacts of this are vast, from reduced confidence, which relate to all facets of life like happiness and success, to reducing your time to search for your purpose. We should be proud and honoured by our differences and thankful, as our combinations of genetic and environmental factors are not present in any other being. It is easy to be someone else, which is very common. It requires no effort as we act like monkeys; the "monkey see monkey do" attitude.

It takes courage to be who we are. It is linked to our traits. We should not just accept our children for who they are but provide them with opportunities to build their self-confidence. It is also

---

Day 63: *Everyone goes through hard times at some point; soften it #HardYards*

Day 64: *Spend a night with the homeless and try to understand the struggles they endure on a daily basis #SleepWithTheHomeless*

important to socialise them, so they learn to communicate and respect people who are different to themselves. These social opportunities will allow them to embrace and be proud of who they are and similarly accept others for who they are.

Sometimes people attempt to set a new precedent. Without even contemplating the potential positive outcomes, society refuses to give it a stamp of approval. Lift people up; don't bring them down. Life would be boring if we were all the same. There would be no excitement. One of the aims of reproduction is genetic variation. We should embrace being different, not just biologically, but in every way highlighted above.

We search for our partners and though we say, "We want someone like us", that is impossible, technically, and we end up compromising and loving the person for who they are because we forget that we all are unique despite the religion or culture we follow. All of us have compatible partners, whether it is based on personal traits, common interests, attraction or culture. Opposites attract, like people repel; it's basic physics. I believe that all partners are potentially compatible since we are not alike.

Though people share more similarities than differences and are 98% identical to our closest relatives, the chimpanzees; that 2% difference is enough to make us unique. Many factors such as genetic makeup and environment contribute to this variation between individuals.

Viewing individuals as unique is good! Trying to be other people through social media or with plastic surgery indirectly suggests that we are probably not comfortable with who we are. I am not against plastic surgery as some of the medical approaches are beneficial in helping us survive. Be who you are, for who you are, is the best that you can be. Be the best version of yourself.

Day 65: Bring a fulfilling end to the week for someone #Week-end
Day 66: Provide a complimentary industry consult #FreeConsult

Build upon characteristics. Being who you are is easier than being someone you are not. You are more comfortable and content with your life. Acceptance is difficult, but it takes time and practice. If you care what others think, then you will be depressed. If we were all the same, then genetically, we would all not exist.

Even twins are different.

We adapt and look at situations differently. This chapter shows us that individuality and variation are endless. The moment we are scared of ourselves is the moment we lose our individuality, which is our best asset in the world. We can use our individuality as a tool to cultivate our inherent strengths, thereby going on a road to probable success. It is boring to be like someone else.

A friend I knew never fitted in with the crowd, but he fitted in his world, and he was happy until it started depressing him that he was so different and that he was not accepted. He was misunderstood, judged and never given a chance. He met a lot of people in life, and at first there was acceptance, until they wanted him to change.

He met someone else, and although she was cautious, she accepted him for who he was. She understood him as she was in a similar position. It can be lonely out there, but there will be people who are like you; patience is the key. Even if it takes your whole life to find your life partner, it's alright. As my professor once said: "Tasty wine takes time to brew in the cellar" – not that I would know in the literal sense, but figuratively, it made a lot of sense.

People view things differently and will tend to be with the people that see things from the same point of view as them – this is rare, but it is possible. Friends have interests; partners have them as well. We will all never have the same amount. It will be different; we may have the same interests but not the same knowledge. Just like our appearance – we may have different ideas on what is appealing.

Day 67: *Teach the simplest things to someone, even if it's learning how to spell his or her name #SimpleTeaching*

Day 68: *Give an Eid gift to someone in need #Eid*

An important aspect of our individuality is a branch of science called hermeneutics. It's not necessarily a science but rather a school of thought which believes that we all have different interpretations of everything. Now back to the science part: why is it that we have so many ideas on the same piece of knowledge or evidence? Hermeneutics explains that. We all think differently due to our vast knowledge, existence, and experiences. One will see that consequently, we can have different points of view on beauty, which was talked about previously, but more of a debatable topic, is the different views on what is deemed intelligent and what is not.

Time alone defines you and allows you to find yourself and be an individual. Sometimes you need to be alone, to reflect on your life and who you are before you can move forward. This is often hard to do, but there comes a point when you realise that it needs to be done otherwise other people besides yourself will get hurt unnecessarily.

We are often so scared of the unknown or losing someone that it holds us back from finding ourselves, which in a way is selfish, for that person needs to grow as well.

Reflection is the best way to maturity and finding out your purpose. Go out with your family and spend time with them; that is when you discover yourself, and not when you sit in front of the television, computer or doing work. It's the quiet or uncommon moments that define who you are. Finding who you are, serves as a critical component to knowing who you are, and saying: "I am who I am".

Day 69: Assist a matriculant or student #Student
Day 70: Give a shoebox of basic essentials to someone in need #Shoebox
Day 71: Give someone else your parking spot. Patience is a virtue #ParkingSpot

5
Character is the Basis of All Actions

As highlighted earlier, we are all unique in our own way even though we are related through our genetic code – there is always some aspect of individuality. We can also share some individuality with others by sharing the same viewpoints.

Nevertheless, the combination of all your characteristics makes you an individual that is unique and different from the person next to you. There are many types of characteristics, and they can be categorised in different fields. The first characteristic that stares you in the face is your physical characteristics. These are brought about mainly by your genetic makeup.

You can't change your physical appearance; if you did, some would agree that you are changing the gifts that were given to you by God. Characteristics come with their disadvantages so why fight over what is socially acceptable. My motto is that being unique enables you to be free and be who you are, and not someone that you're not – this is integral.

Emotional characteristics are from the heart, which is really from your brain. It associates the heart with emotions as it is a symbol of love. To be empathetic, humble, gentle, humane – all these characteristics are difficult to find, as we as humans, generally tend to be selfish, and are all in it for ourselves to win it. Sadly, some realise

---

Day 72: Share some words of wisdom #Wisdom
Day 73: Do a raffle to raise funds for the underprivileged #Raffle
Day 74: Provide a career mentorship workshop #CareerMentorship

this too late after they have done something wrong and then they want to change who they are emotionally as well. Yes, it is possible to change if we really want to, but it is more difficult to let go of old habits.

That's the bottom line.

We grow up a certain way, and we develop habits; a habit of ridiculing another. We choose that, but that is not who we are. We are not born that way. There are many reasons why we are the way we are, but it is more of a notion of social acceptance and not wanting to be different. We don't have the courage to change although if we start embracing and practising changing our habits, it becomes much easier.

Have the courage to be yourself and others will accept and respect you for who you are and may even learn from you.

The presence of a heart doesn't take a lot; the misconception that we need money, is frivolous. We need time, as well as the passion and willingness to sacrifice in order to give back to others from what we have gained. It is not something we see every day. Yes, we all need to earn a living, but helping our fellow human beings is fulfilling. Charles Darwin's theory of natural selection states that the strong survive and the weak don't, purely because they can't adapt.

Whichever way you want to see it, the way I see it is that they can't adapt because we leave them behind to fend for themselves, not realising that we all start somewhere and we all go through hardships. Even for those who were fortunate enough to be born into money/royalty etc., someone must have started somewhere to get them to where they are today.

If we can change the way we see things, life would be that much more enjoyable and fun. Help someone, be different, for those are

---

Day 75: Provide a time management workshop #TimeManagement
Day 76: Motivate and mentor someone during their studies #InvestInTheYouth

the characteristics you don't inherit and don't see every day.

Spirituality is linked to our emotions. The way we lead our lives, our way of life, is linked to who we are to a certain extent. Religions that encourage and have charity as their way of life, help us to become better people. However, they also stop us from being who we are as certain characteristics are socially acceptable and others are not.

There is a fine line between being who you are and not being responsible. For example, smoking or drinking, are not genetic characteristics, but behavioural, emotional and spiritual. Harming yourself is never being who you are. Think about it. All those vices lead to a different set of editing your characteristics. I suppose this creates variation, right? Wrong, all genes determine that, as well as your environment. Look at your characteristics, and what you can improve on, for tomorrow you will be gone, and you don't want to be living in regret.

We all have choices, right or wrong. The trick is to get back on the right path. We should assert ourselves with good thoughts only from good people and educate ourselves. We all look for partners and what we want in them but look at yourself first. Change for the better and because you want to, not because you have to as someone tells you to. Be your own person.

Characteristics, therefore, don't define us; our actions and intentions do.

Some characteristics cannot be given and some you are naturally more confident with. Some are adaptations. It is a set of skills. These ultimately shape your character. Verily, character forms the basis of all actions.

Day 77-80: *The best among you are those who learn and then teach it to others #Learn&Teach*

Day 81: *Teach kids on the street a thing or two; they need our support #StreetSmart*

6
Adapting to Environments

The measure to which we adapt is a skill whether acquired or not, but it is the one skill that is essential to life. Organisms adapt to their environment, and whether you believe in evolution or not, humans adapt by changing their attitude and perceptions of that environment. Some go as far as physical changes, but it is mostly emotional changes.

Change is good; new environment, new habitat or new anything is good. It challenges the mind and body to survive. It keeps us healthy. Activity keeps us healthy by exercising all facets of our brains. 'Survival of the fittest', so Charles Darwin would say, but it is true in the case of humans. If we don't adapt, we won't live happy lifestyles and nor can we be successful. It is not easy as I said before; it is a skill. When we are repeatedly exposed to different situations, our tendency to adapt more quickly increases. This is not to say it gets easier. We just handle the situation better knowing how to enter and survive in a different adaptation.

Adaptation has been going on for years; it is why we have survived. In life, we are not hardwired to know how to deal with situations or live in certain environments and yet we must deal with the curveballs that are thrown at us, good or bad. This is what makes us humans and so complex; we apply our knowledge, skills

Day 82: Co-ordinate an event to make people laugh sustainably #Laugh
Day 83: Feed an animal #FeedAnimals

and experiences that we are fortunate enough to be able to develop to the various situations we face.

There are some cases where we need to adapt so much that we just give up. This is evidence that change, though good, is also challenging and frustrating. When we are born, we have to adapt to the world. First, our eyes adapt to the world followed by our bodies. Adaptation does not come naturally.

I believe more exposure to various situations makes it easier and different influences also help us deal with adaptation. As a child, certain help is given to us such as how to adapt to the world through advice, practise and observation. For example, toilet training, where a younger sister may learn from observing her older sister. This just shows the ease at which children can adapt.

Apart from physical adaptation, there is also personal adaptation where we have to find ourselves ultimately out in the world. It is not easy to adapt socially when we have our own opinions and attitudes. We are often shielded by our parents when we shouldn't be protected so closely. We need room to grow a thick skin which can only happen by being thrown out in the deep end and by experience. Children who are left on their own, grow up independently which is a vital skill to working on their own and excelling in life. Parents cannot hold our hands forever; we need to fly free as a bird.

This can be linked to characteristics. Certain characteristics, genetically inherited, allow us to adapt faster and much better than others. For example, research has shown that birth order is related to leadership roles. The firstborn is more likely to adapt faster as he or she is born a natural leader.

With adaptation comes either being a leader or a follower. Are you a shepherd or are you a sheep? We can't all be shepherds, nor all sheep. There has to be both for the cycle of life to take place.

Day 84: Give your competitor the upper-hand, even if they are direct competitors and in the same market as you are #KindCompetitor

Day 85: Randomly compliment someone for no reason and brighten up their day #Compliment

Whichever you choose, your life is in your hands, as how you choose to adapt is up to you, but the more effectively you do it, the better quality of life you will have.

A leader has the necessary skills to lead a group of people to either greatness (success) or failure. The level of achievement of leaders is measured by their success in all facets to lead a team and leave a legacy behind. The men and women at the top of businesses fulfil these criteria. They can adapt to different needs while still facing the challenges of standing on their own two feet as well as leading other people.

We go through phases in our lives where we adapt from being children to adults and then sub-divisions of adulthood and teenagers. Exposure to different situations tests our adaptation abilities. There is no certain way to adapt easily. We gain the necessary skills to help us, but they don't apply to different situations.

Animals' lives are put at risk if they cannot adapt to their environment. We are fortunate in that our bodies enable us to physically adapt using complex systems. We adapt daily to the climate and environment. There are needs for long-term and short-term adaptations, for example, a new job, a new location and new friends.

We say we acquire a taste for something; this is adapting to the specific item. For example, sushi is an acquired taste. You learn to adapt to eat it. If shown how by your parents or friends, it is easier to enjoy and increase the quality of life. If not, you hate the taste. The first experience can be bad, but you learn to adapt. My first experience was bad with sushi, but now I love it.

Not all will like it, and that's okay. We all won't adapt, and it's a test for us to challenge ourselves. We can if we really want to and make an effort. If our lives depend on it, we will. It is part of reproduction and increasing the population. Characteristics we shy away

---

Day 86: Nature conservation is very important, protect and preserve it #NatureConservation

Day 87: Hydrate someone on a hot day #Hydration

from are less prone to adaptation, but it is essential for life.

Employers look for the ability to adapt in people they interview for jobs. It is a good asset and skill to have.

Mandela adapted to his cell. He was patient. It eventually led to his freedom. If his heart was not in the right place, along with other incredible virtues, it might have never led to a long walk to freedom. Therefore, our country might have been different.

Freedom was fought for in this country and was achieved in 1994. As human beings we also have freedom but when does it begin? That was an important question growing up. We yearn for the authority to be our own boss, but when that time does come, it is so much more than what we expect. Freedom can be a good or bad thing. In the world, it is good as we learn to survive on our own which is linked to adaptation.

Given freedom, we can practise adaptation. We learn to survive on our own and stand on our own two feet. It can be bad when that freedom happens too early before we have been instilled with the necessary skills of life. When this happens, we are more likely to explore the less desirable things in life, taking the wrong path. This is likely to happen of our own accord or through our parents. It could be from our parents' "hold"; the discipline they use to control us that restricts freedom from which we yearn to break free.

Some can manage and adapt, but others potentially end up going downhill. From a parent's point of view, to give freedom is difficult as they know the reality of this earth and all it entails. They try to protect us, but some parents give too much freedom while others don't give any at all. This is both detrimental and beneficial to the child.

This is where good morals and understanding come in which goes hand-in-hand with the freedom they are given. We all want to

---

Day 88: Conduct a presentation to teach something exciting and intriguing to others #Presentation

Day 89: Conduct a seminar to teach new things to a group of people #Seminar

be our children's best friend, but some don't separate that barrier, and that is where the problem arises.

Be it a child, parent, ordinary citizen or sports player, adaptation is relative. It is human nature to allow for one important variable to allow for efficient adaptation: time. With time, there is also place. The perfect combination of time and place allows a living organism (both man and animal) to adapt to its respective environment.

Day 90: Give a lift to someone in need #LiftSomeone
Day 91: Provide a long-term approach that can help society in any field #Approach
Day 92: Catch up and take friends out for ice cream #Ice-Cream

7
Why Intelligence Doesn't Make You Successful

Although adaptation of living organisms takes place through a degree of freedom, the true essence of intelligence and success can also be experienced when people are free.

We are all born with a brain. How we utilise it though, is different. Keeping the brain stimulated leads to a healthier lifestyle. Stimulating that brain from a young age helps with coping at school and excelling. The issue comes in when we determine what intelligence is and who decides this. This is the key issue in our schools today.

We have a curriculum that states what is intelligent and what is not. What promotes you and what does not and that tells us whether you are stupid or not. No one is stupid; it is just that we all utilise our brain cells differently.

Most of us, perhaps, don't utilise our full brain capacity. Different parts are stimulated more than others depending on our interests and capabilities. It's interesting to note that in South African schools, we perform the worst in the world in mathematics and science. Most think it is because they are stupid. I think it's the other way around.

Day 93: *Contribute towards a campaign where the deaf are able to also go to the movies and watch it in subtitles #Accessibility*

Day 94: *Provide academic mentorship to university and collegiate students #AcademicMentorship*

Society deems what is intelligent and what is not, and if you do not fall into that category, you will fail. Another fact is the language barrier. As soon as we cannot communicate in English, we are perceived as dumb, because it is seen as universal language. Who made English the dominant language? In addition, schools seldom emphasise critical thinking. This is key. These are some of the issues that we are faced with today with regards to our intelligence, and these could also speak to other countries despite their unique circumstances.

My grades were just above average in school. Does that make me less intelligent? I wasn't a particular fan of the schooling system. To this day, most schools adopt a generic approach to a variety of unique scholars. This is problematic.

We can't really say that school is paramount where it is clustered as a group because it is convenient to teach all in the same class, in the same uniform, with the same time periods. This model is a business. Universities are businesses too, but their one fundamental difference is independence.

At universities no one is treated like sheep. Rather, they groom them in becoming shepherds of their own sheep by promoting a distinct line of thinking, critique and application. I am not saying we should do away with the schooling system. There are fantastic schools out there that have groomed and developed pioneers and immaculate leaders today. What I am saying is that more time should be allocated towards assisting pupils individually. Qualitative and individualistic educational approaches are critical for the growth and development of our country.

Also, we should teach pupils virtues and values, without dictation. Allow them to make mistakes and educate them on the reasons why it was wrong. Don't prevent mistakes; you don't learn that way.

Day 95: Buy drinks for policemen #Policemen
Day 96: Spend time and give an ear to the elderly #ListenToTheElderly
Day 97: Help someone with their shopping #ShoppingHelp

When someone puts their hand in the fire for the first time, they won't do it again. Similarly, learners (as well as animals who are also intelligent in their own right), won't do it again if they see that the consequences were severe or not adequate. Most South Africans are creative. We have to work with their creativity. This is an asset to have, especially when we are living in such a digital and innovative age.

I will use two schools of thought when it comes to intelligence. Howard Gartner's multiple levels of intelligence are more appealing to me, and I find it makes more sense than Bloom's taxonomy of a single intelligence level comprising of different attributes.

The people who succeed are able to adapt to society and its ways that are deemed correct and with what success entails. Those who do not succeed, don't necessarily fail but instead choose a different pathway. Having a job is a form of success although to some it is not seen this way.

We can't change who we are nor can we change the past. Different fields of expertise involve multiple levels of intelligence. For example, accountants are involved in numbers and rationality, working with figures and deductive reasoning. They don't necessarily memorise things like doctors have to during their studies.

What about musicians? There is a level of intelligence, multiple levels of intelligence in fact. Soon we need to reach a level of balance. Balance in the form of merit, not class or background. In South Africa, I don't think we are there yet, but we are striving in working towards that.

Matric is everything as it determines your entry into university or the world of work. Great, so you get accepted and then we see this trend of students dropping out. Why? They can't adapt or handle the pressure, but their results speak otherwise.

Day 98: *Support your mentor during a challenging period #SupportYourMentor*

Day 99: *Support those making an honest living through creativity, innovation and talent, instead of fuelling poverty that could adversely increase crime #HonestLiving*

This shows that excellent marks are both a sign and not a sign of intelligence. Intelligence is common sense, deductive reasoning, being able to adapt and go beyond the textbook. Being a school student is so different to being a university student. There is a culmination of social intelligence, emotional intelligence and not just intellectual intelligence. That is the problem we face. Excellent marks do not determine intelligence. We have to conform to ideas in school that we don't agree with to excel because we know that if we don't, we will get left behind. It is a strange society that we live in. Sad but true.

We send out children to these fancy schools hoping to give them the best education, but it is what they make of it. You can give them everything, take the horse to the water, but you can't make it drink the water nor can you force a learner to study. They must put in the effort. The motivation to study is there for some, but others lack it which is what we need to focus on.

Being knowledgeable is not intelligence. You can know everything, but if you can't apply it in the real world, then you know nothing. Our parents never went to school, or some didn't finish. We tend to think they know nothing when in fact they made a life for themselves. They are probably more intelligent than us. We rely on technology these days – how are we using it?

Being intelligent is to teach someone else. We all have our opinions – and this is mine. We are all intelligent in one form or another. We display it differently, and we should put the effort in and stimulate our brains.

Our brains are like appliances. We need fuel which is food like machines need electricity to operate. If we don't use the appliance, it gets old and rusty. Likewise, if we don't use our brains, we become old before our time. It is so important to stimulate the brain with a

---

Day 100: *Donate old clothes to those in need #OldClothes*
Day 101: *Show gratitude and appreciation to those who have supported you in any sphere of your life #Appreciation*

number of brain games or numerical activities.

Your job does not define your intelligence; we have different interests and one is not better than the other as all are intertwined. Much emphasis is placed on doctors and nurses as they save lives. There's nothing wrong with an accountant, teacher, or policeman. The one saves you money, the other prepares you for life, and the world out there and another prevents potential dangers.

Which is better?

We need all of the professions. If you look at it, we take a further step in the interest to become an expert or specialist in that field. We have these fancy titles, but we are every profession – just an expert with that degree.

Speaking about experts.

There is also something called 10,000 hours.

There is a theory that says 10,000 hours makes one an expert in one's required field. In other words, it would take one 10,000 hours to become proficient and excel at what one does. Five years is said to be the equivalent of 10,000 hours, with approximately 2,000 hours per year, making it close to 170 hours per month and that works out to around 40 hours per week. How many of us are proficient and excel at each hour of work we do? How many of us take 25-30 hours to do a week's task as opposed to 40 hours of an average individual?

Working smart instead of working hard may work for some, but for others, they may be governed by their daily hours. Now let's take a typical day's work encompassing a lunch break meeting or two, time on emails or social media, etc. If we subtract these activities, you would only get 25-30 hours out of 40 hours of proficient work completed in a week.

This is also dependent on the type of work or area of expertise

---

Day 102: *Persons with a disability do not infer an inability #Ability*
Day 103: *Provide awareness and support for those with Osgood-Schlatters #OsgoodSchlatters*

one is in which would require various demands and deadlines to meet. For example, a street hawker has been working for more than 20 years to support his family, through constant hardship and patience. Do we call him/her an expert street hawker? A sports player plays professionally for ten years, and he is regarded as an expert on television.

The point is: we need to differentiate between an expert and someone who is experienced. Therefore, one could argue that the street hawker and sports player are experienced at what they do. They are available to offer their advice, based on their experiences. As my brother says: "Experience, no textbook can teach you. One has to experience it for themselves." How does one become an expert? Are expertise and experience the same? Surely not!

A student studies for six years (120 hours) to become a doctor. Is he or she now an expert doctor? Five years of deliberate, engaged and thorough focus as well as more experience after graduating would make him an expert, depending on the specialty and sub-specialty he or she chooses.

There is also a notion that it would take 1,000 hours of research to complete a Master's degree. The average time students take to complete their Masters is said to be approximately two years. If two years give you 2,000 hours, why has someone taken so long to complete their Masters if the suggested time is 1,000 hours? Surely it would then take them six months? Yes, research is a different process. There are constraints of trial and error, submissions, protocols, field work, etc. However, is the Master's candidate now not an expert? Remember in the clinical and academic sense, an expert should do a minimum of five year's work experience after graduation.

Similarly, let's look at professional sports players. It is deliberated

---

Day 104: *Your country is not just a beautiful land; it is your people that make it even more breathtaking #Country*

Day 105: *Our youth is the greatest investment for our country #Youth*

that if one wants to be a good sportsman or sportswoman, they would need to be practising or working hard at their game for a minimum of 10,000 hours.

Let's remember the 40 hour/week formula for daily workers. A child or adolescent only gets up to 20 hours of sports practice per week (that's if the child is attending school, of course). Therefore, a child/adolescent would need to skip school to become a good player in five years.

In Europe, there are soccer schools where the focus is both on academics and soccer, but there is more emphasis on the sport which gives them an opportunity to excel at the sport. Then again, some players in developing countries have minimal time to practice and are in worse conditions and hardship.

Yet, some of these disadvantaged players are still able to come out on top compared to other countries. Why? It can't just be raw talent. The 10,000 hours formula is not a one-size-fits-all approach; it is hugely dependent on the field one works in, the sport played, the individual and demands of the job. Furthermore, working smart over working hard is the best philosophy to empower a qualitative approach rather than a quantitative approach to approximately 10,000 hours of expertise.

Verily:

- Work smart, until it is proficient, not done.
- Train hard, challenge like a king and win like a champion.
- Intelligence is a relative, qualitative concept that can't be tested with inductive reasoning.

Day 106: *As we engage with communities on our journey towards making a sustainable difference, it is often the many smiles that touch our hearts despite their circumstances including those who graciously give their time for free #TogetherWeAreStronger*

Day 107: *Nurture and care for the soil – the nourishment of the earth #Soil*

8
THE ENEMY

There are a number of people who have inspired me throughout my career, namely: Tim Noakes, Nelson Mandela and Bruce Lee. I grew up watching Bruce Lee's movies and the second movie I ever watched growing up when I was six years old was *Enter the Dragon*, the first being *Aladdin*.

Enter the Dragon was an interesting movie. I watched it as a child because I loved Bruce Lee's martial arts, karate kicks and watched some episodes at home. My brother introduced me to Bruce Lee and other martial arts movies, and for this, I will always be grateful. When the movie was released, I was really keen to watch it. When I watched it with my sister, I realised that the themes were based on his life as an inspiring journey.

There is one snippet from that movie where there is a monster that haunts him in his dreams. I was scared when I watched it at the cinema, and I had a riveting nightmare the next day, which was similar to that dragon or monster from the movie.

I woke up at home with a huge shock, and I was crying a lot. My dad and mum consoled me, and I ended up sleeping in their room. My brother and sister also came from their rooms and thought that I had got hurt. It was bad, and they wondered why I was crying so much. I told them it was a dream about a monster. We all thought that it was just a once off occurrence and I eventually went back to sleep.

Day 108: Don't underestimate any of your inherent strengths #InherentStrengths
Day 109: Violence and abuse are precursors of someone's mindset #PeacefulMindset

A year or two after that I dreamt of the monster again, and it was worse. The third time I dreamt of the monster, it was equally bad, but by then I was nine or ten years old. Today, I still dream of that monster and probably dream of him once or twice a year. As I eventually got older, I got less scared, possibly because I got used to this monster or dragon, or I developed a better emotional intelligence and became more mature to deal with it.

In the dreams, the monster is not attacking me and is just there in the dreams. I'm not sure if it was a message for my life that "keeping your enemies close" was a bad thing as that is what this monster was possibly telling me from a young age.

It could also be telling me something different; I am not 100% sure. It started on a bad note but maybe ended off on a good note. I wouldn't say that we are necessarily close, but I would say that he is not harmful and when I see him in my dreams I am no longer scared but I do get the shivers. I am definitely no longer afraid, as I remember how I used to feel growing up as a child.

I keep on thinking as I evolve that I never did well in school but always progressed slowly through life, and I never progressed in certain areas of my life. I think the dragon was there and was scary as I slowly progressed in school but as soon as I progressed in life, the dragon became less harmful. Now he is at that point where he doesn't seem harmful at all, and I am even more progressive in life. Yes, I am a scientist, but I am also a firm believer in dreams just like many other people and scientists. I believe they are there as messages to either tell you of the unknown or some 'omens' which could have meaning to your life.

When I was in school, my progression was ordinary while most of my peers had extraordinary progress. I continued to work hard and never to give up, and fortunately, after school, my progress

---

Day 110: Devote your time and effort to a charity
and hospice doing remarkable work #Hospice

Day 111: Conserving nature is the most imperative act we can do for
our environment, including on our beaches #ConserveNature

was better, while most of my peers' progress started to plateau or decline. The below figures show my particular progress (Figure A) as compared to the average person (Figure B) who did well at school. The lesson from the below figures is that consistency is key. Persevere and look ahead despite the obstacles and enemies you may encounter.

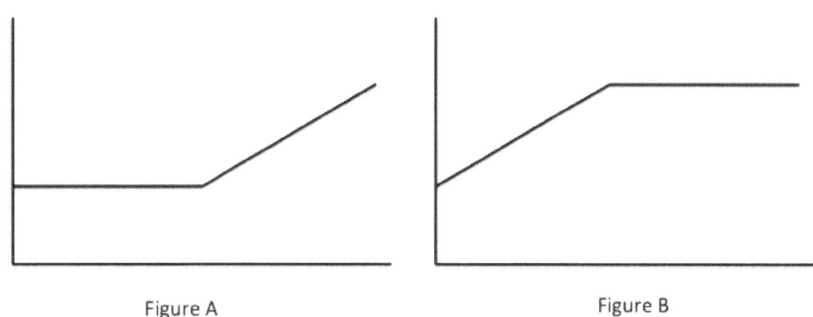

Figure A   Figure B

I am not sure if the monster will come to the point where he will be friendly, and I will be successful, but that is the end of it. It all comes back to the man in the movie, Bruce Lee. Although a headache pill killed him, it was documented in a number of documentaries that he was also killed by the jealousy and narcissism of the Western world.

I am not sure where my life is going but I have a huge feeling that by the age of 32 or 33, similar to Bruce Lee, jealousies might affect me and when they do, this monster is going to be friendlier. Both of these two terms have been intertwined and termed in that as a child, jealousy was not there, but the enemy was, and later on in life, the enemy is not there, but jealousy is.

The enemy is not killing me, but is the jealousy? Jealousy is everywhere. Most people see your successes as their failures. I

Day 112: Practise tolerance – it cultivates patience which promotes peace #Tolerance
Day 113: Devote your time to human rights and uplifting the youth #HumanRights
Day 114: Surprise someone on their birthday, even if you don't know them #Birthday

have always questioned that, why? We all have a similar platform to start from but have different paths, as mentioned in an earlier chapter. That will always be my concern, i.e. is my life similar to that of the life Bruce Lee lived?

We were on the same platform with different skills, his being martial arts and mine something else, but will I die for different reasons? I look up to him and often think about him. Although I admire his wife's outlook on celebrating his life and not questioning his death, I often wonder what he would have achieved, had he still been alive.

Summary

On a daily basis, we deal with enemies either because they want to be closer to us or they try and want to bring us down. People have been trying to get me down while I progress and that is exactly what happened to Bruce. He progressed so much, but people tried to bring him down.

It wasn't the enemy that was trying to kill him but rather the people around him and I think the enemy that he had with him throughout his life was a sign. For me, I don't know if it's also a sign because still today I dream of that monster. The monster is brown-maroon in colour, very tainted and an unnatural colour with red eyes.

It is scary, but because I am used to it, I no longer flinch nor cringe.

The other thing that I dream a lot of and which people consider a bad omen is of snakes. I dream of snakes in different colours, yellow, green and it freaks me out. I know that when I dream of this, it is a

---

Day 115: *Promote the use of philosophy – this improves thinking among others #Philosophy*
Day 116: *Don't underestimate what kindness can do to someone #BeKind*

possible sign of current enemies that are looking at me.

When I dream of the other enemy, it is a sign of the possible progression that I am experiencing in my life. Through dreams, we learn to take note of the signs. I certainly do because it has affected me since I was a young child. Through life, we later understand (or try to) what those signs mean.

Eventually.

PART 2
THE SUPERIOR VENA CAVA

9
Education

When growing up, I developed a murmur of the heart. This is the irony of life – the fact that this book is called *Heart* and the fact that I was also announced Mr Heart South Africa. I used to find it difficult to breathe at times and couldn't walk long distances. I had also developed exercise-induced asthma and was on a pump.

Playing sports at school helped my heart health, and I slowly got weaned off the asthma pump. My siblings always motivated me to get up and do something and created an atmosphere of enjoyment where we would play either cricket or soccer on the road in the neighbourhood. At that time, there were no cell phones or advanced digital technology. Recreation, sport and picnics were the cool things.

Pre-primary and Primary School

I attended Seko Medsi Nursery School. I wasn't fond of it. I never wanted to sit down with the other children. From young, I wanted to be stimulated on my own, and I got bored very quickly. While the other children were doing activities, I was either daydreaming or yawning because I grasped the concept, the story or the activity the first time already.

I later did nursery schooling with my mom at home. I then went to pre-school at Crown Reef Primary School in Crown Mines. Pre-school also wasn't enjoyable for me. I used to wait long hours for my dad to come pick me up from school. It wasn't easy at that time. Both my parents were working long hours at the Bruma Flea Market while my sister was either finishing high school or at Wits University. My brother had schooled in Durban and used to come home for the holidays.

Pre-school went by pretty quickly though, and I then went to E.P. Baumann Primary School where I completed Grades 1 to 4. Being independent from a young age, where I liked to do my own thing, served its purpose in Grade 3. Just like most other schools, there is a merit and demerit system. In Grade 3, our teachers would give us merits based on any independent work we would do.

These entailed writing short stories on anything interesting or what we had done over the past weekends. I enjoyed writing and reflecting on interesting things. In 1997 during my Grade 3 year, I was awarded a scroll by the school. A certificate was 200 merits. A medal was 400 merits. A trophy was 600 merits, and a scroll was 800 merits.

To this day, I can't find that scroll, but that was the most memorable moment of E.P. Baumann Primary School. This award had ingrained a long-term self-esteem in me and motivated me to always be independent and productive in everything that I do.

In 1998, my sister graduated from Wits University as a Speech Therapist and Audiologist. She got a job at St. Vincent's School for the Deaf.

My mom put me into a school near to St. Vincent's so that I could stay with my sister and so that she wouldn't stay alone. I didn't like this idea because I was going to miss my friends from E.P. Baumann

---

Day 121: *We know that living financially responsible is the key to success #FinanciallyResponsible*

Day 122: *Hardship is designed to make you stronger, not weaker. Easy is designed to make you weaker, not stronger #EmbraceChallenges*

and didn't want to adjust to another school. I am glad I did though. I went to Rosebank Primary School.

The amazing thing about Rosebank Primary was that it had sports. E.P. Baumann lacked somewhat in that department. My passion and love for cricket was then developed at Rosebank Primary and no longer in the park or on the street. It was here, at the age of 10, where I got to experience hard-ball cricket for the first time.

I am so grateful that I went to Rosebank Primary. Our principal, Mr Les Lambert, was awesome. He continuously promoted academic excellence, sports participation and etiquette. Our school motto was: "Manners Maketh Man". Without a doubt, the pupils lived up to this motto.

I loved my time at school because when going back to St. Vincent, it was a test of patience. I was grateful that I had a place to sleep and a plate of food to eat. But it took a while to get used to hostel food and live in a flat where there was no television or time with my brother. I loved being with my sister, we had so much fun, but I missed home in Homestead Park.

We would go and visit on weekends, and I couldn't wait for those moments. We termed it "party house" – and St. Vincent's flat was patient house. St. Vincent's was also a school for the deaf. I, therefore, got to learn sign language through the students that I used to play sport with. In this way, I developed an empathy for students with hearing disabilities without even realising it.

Today I still use some sign language, but I have forgotten a lot because I stopped communicating in sign language when I went to high school. What an experience, when I look back on it, I don't regret going to Rosebank. I will always fondly remember those times that my sister would go to The Zone at Rosebank to buy groceries, and she would come back with my favourite – chocolate doughnuts

---

Day 123: *They will criticise you and underestimate your potential. It is your responsibility to show them your worth and what you are capable of #KnowYourWorth*

Day 124: *Capture a moment that will last a lifetime #LifeMoment*

(no longer a favourite!)

Thanks, Khatija and Mom! This is where my passion for cricket was ignited, where I got to learn sign language and where I got to eat mulberries every morning when walking to school from St. Vincent. Wearing white school shirts with mulberry stains, which have never come off and are still there today – the proof is there!

My sister played an integral role in my early years of childhood. She instilled some discipline into her young brother, but she was also very loving and caring. I remember fondly when she allocated a portion from her salary at the time towards my Kumon education. Kumon was a Japanese form of tutoring that enhanced pupils' skills in Mathematics and English.

Kumon ranges from primary school level right up to university level. It is widely used today. I recall during this time of doing Kumon (1999-2001), I held the record in South Africa for doing the timetables the fastest. Now this accolade is purely my father's. I remember at the dinner table that my dad would continuously probe me on different timetables – "9x9? 8x13? 7x9?" and so on and so on. There was a timetables book that they had bought for me from Checkers which cost three rands. I used to learn that, and after learning that book, I went back to my dad.

My dad was either a clothing representative or salesman, and he was very good with numbers and calculations. He should have become an accountant and not a cricketer! That's why he always wanted me to do well at school while playing sports. My dad continuously tested my timetable skills.

This test then ventured into school. In school, I was on a higher level than my class with timetables. We used to play a cowboy game. We would go up to the front of the class, in pairs of two, facing our backs to each other. Our teacher would call out a sum, and one of

---

Day 125: *Words of wisdom are not merely for encouragement but also serve as a beacon for action #wisdom*
Day 126: *Be steady and firm in all your actions, even if your greatest fear or obstacles are in front of you #OvercomeYourFears*

us would then turn around and "shoot" the other person calling out the answer.

Every time, I had "shot" each member in my class. Timetables were my strength, and as a result, in Grade 5, I was invited to write the Maths Olympiad. I was the only Grade 5 pupil, and the rest were Grades 6 and 7 pupils. I found the Olympiad tough and I didn't do well, but I was humbled to have been invited to participate.

This was as a result of Kumon – it taught pupils to finish their work quickly yet effectively. Till today, people ask, how did you complete a number of tasks in such a short space of time? I would like to acknowledge the following people: Mrs Roos for rewarding us with merits when we did independent work in Grade 3. The result was that I got the highest merits in school and ingrained a high sense of independent work from a young age. In addition, my sister for allowing me to attend Kumon. This allowed me to practise time management between school work, Kumon and sports and to do all three efficiently and effectively.

Islamic Boarding School (2004)

I was a tad disappointed when my mother moved me from E.P. Baumann Primary School to Rosebank Primary School. However, I was later grateful about that move because it allowed me to be introduced to sport and cricket on a better level. Then, after Grade 9 in 2004, my mother wanted to move me into an Islamic boarding school, for an Islamic studies year.

The main reason for wanting me to go to boarding school was for the memorisation of the Quran. I was doing it at high school and unfortunately, because of school, and cricket, it was not allowing me the time to focus on it as effectively or exclusively as I would have wanted to. She felt that those who did devote their time to the memorisation of the Quran in its entirety had to be disciplined in such a way that you had to spend a lot more time and wake up at certain times in order to achieve this penultimate achievement – the memorisation of God's words. What can be greater than this? Nothing beats that in Islam.

Being at home was not the ideal environment for me to do so. There are quite a number of Islamic boarding schools around the world that cater for this and allow you to memorise the Quran effectively.

Eventually, my mother identified a boarding school, and she motivated me to go. I remember quite fondly that my brother was not too happy about the decision as it would serve as a brief interruption in my high school years in terms of rhythm and I too was not happy about it purely because of the interruptions it might cause and having to adapt to another environment. I also didn't want to move schools again.

I had already adapted from E.P. Baumann Primary School to Rosebank Primary School and then from Rosebank Primary into a high school, and now from a high school to going out of the schooling system to a boarding school purely for religious studies. In terms of adapting to another environment and being away from home, that was a bit of a concern for me.

I didn't like the idea that my mother wanted me to do that full time. What initially persuaded me to go was when the principal of the institution informed me that there were cricket facilities and that the boys played cricket often – that caught my attention. I think my mom knew how to soften me up.

The principal said very confidently: "Bring your pads and bat, they play cricket," as he shook his head and smiled from ear to ear. I responded with a smile and asked: "Really?" He said: "Yes, most definitely!"

I stayed, but eventually realised that it was tape-ball cricket! Tennis balls with masking tape wrapped around them. I chuckled and immediately wanted to go back, even though the aim for going there was for religious studies.

The year went by, and I became a lot stronger, and this was probably the turning point in my life where I was bullied less as I was able to be more sociable and know how to handle myself in contentious situations. Whereas before boarding school I was picked on quite often and from a social perspective, I was extremely quiet and more introverted and reserved.

Boarding school was certainly that kind of platform that allowed me to come out of my shell. Specifically, my confidence levels grew in the sense that they trained us to do a number of talks on religious topics. I recall my first talk on "respect for parents" where I was extremely nervous to the extent where you could even see my pants shivering like it had its own earth tremor.

My anxiety was quite noticeable by a number of my peers at the institution who were listening to my talk at the time. When I did my second talk on "brotherhood" I was still a bit nervous but towards the end of the year, I was able to give a talk with fruition, and I was a lot more confident. That's when my confidence around speaking within social circles peaked. The exposure on a variety of platforms had helped tremendously with confidence, especially when being thrown directly into the deep end.

For me, if I was able to speak or present in front of 200 people at the tender age of 15, talking to 300 people today is no different. My current occupation now as an academic or even doing speaking or

---

Day 132: *We can never be certain of what our future holds but one thing is for sure, we work hard to get somewhere and we work even harder to stay there #SmartWork*

Day 133: *Drink | Educate | Share | Rooibos #Rooibos*

presenting, allows me not only to be confident but also to transcend my values and skills to an array of audiences. I keep questioning myself that if it were not for boarding school and the experience of being in that environment (adapting out of my comfort zone), would I be where I am today?

I thank my mother again as she took me out of an environment and saw that it was not really ideal for me and then put me in another environment where I had to grow and become independent and resilient very quickly.

Whether it was changing schools where I became a fond lover of sports, or whether it was going to a boarding school for religious studies, the one positive that emanated from these years was that I had gained a lot of confidence. I became stronger, and I was more out of my shell when being in social circles.

There were, however, a number of challenges and hardships that I faced at boarding school. One of them obviously being that I was homesick, as this was the first time I was away from home on a permanent basis and being housed at an institution.

We were sharing rooms with four guys and there were two bunk beds, two guys on each bunk bed. At that time there were no cellular phones for most of us guys, and I certainly didn't have one, so I would have to call my family once a week using the office phone. If anything was going on at home, I would not have known about it. I wouldn't say that it was an institutional prison, but I would say that it was a sacrifice that I had to endure for personal development and education.

That was one major sacrifice, but I had to endure others. One of which, was that there were a number of guys who were suffering from tuberculosis (T.B.), and this is a type of disease that is airborne. Whenever I used to walk, I had to cover my nose and mouth in fear

---

Day 134: We need to work together to prevent veld fires #Ceasefires
Day 135: Education is not just a key to success, it is a springboard to unimaginable possibilities #Education

of getting this disease.

During 2004, my brother was doing his medical internship at the Baragwanath Hospital in Johannesburg, and he had always informed us on what to do and how to prevent it. Fortunately, it was not the whole year and it was only noticeable from those who had T.B. during the latter half of the year.

The other challenge that I experienced was from a cultural perspective. It was positive in the sense that there was an array of scholars and students from around the world which allowed me to appreciate, understand and engage with many different people. I developed an understanding of their values and virtues. There were guys from Pakistan, India and England, some countries in Africa and even from America, who came to the institution to do religious studies in Islam. However, never mind being from a different culture, especially the guys from India and Pakistan, the challenge within an Islamic institution was that some of them were homosexual.

Some of the leaders of the institution still don't know to this day that some of the older boys used to go around in the hostels – and I can't find a lighter word than "rape" – and molest the younger boys in the institution.

I obviously thought very defensively and didn't want this to happen to me. We were on a rigid and strict timeline in the institution where we had to wake up before sunrise and sleep at 10 pm with only a tea or lunch break the whole day. I slept with my cricket bat in case one of them came to me in the evening and tried something. I was only 15, and this is why I supposedly thought defensively if something had to happen to me.

Fortunately, nothing transpired, but there were a lot of remarks or attempts of that nature. However, there was no physical contact with anyone. Nevertheless, the sense that I had to live with this

---

Day 136: Give and help from the heart #Heart
Day 137: *When life has your back against the wall, never give up, just turn to the other side and have hope #NeverSayDie*

concern that they would come in the middle of the night, was an inconvenience, for lack of a better word.

Another challenge (from a spiritual perspective), was that I had observed activities of a "Jinn" – supernatural creatures in Arabian mythology, or in broader terms, a demon. There was one occasion where we had come back from our evening class at 9.30 pm, and the door of the hostel and the padlock was broken into.

We had thought that someone had broken into the hostel. But there was no evidence of such or anything of that sort. When we had entered the dormitory, we had heard a number of the guys screaming, and I was shocked as well because when we went into our rooms, we found that all our mattresses, blankets and even padlocks on our cupboards were broken and had been thrown onto the floor.

It was not a pretty sight, and it was something that no one at the institution had ever seen in their five years of being there. When we saw the shocked reaction of one of the senior scholars, we knew that it was a serious occurrence and not to be taken lightly.

We contacted the principal of the institution to come in, and he also, from a spiritual perspective, was quite learned and an expert in that regard. He had asked all of us to leave the dormitory. We were all gathered outside wondering what had happened, what could it have been, what was going to happen to our belongings, as most of it was damaged?

We deliberated outside while they were busy inside. We waited for 20 odd minutes, and before he came out there were a number of screaming monsters; I remember the scream very vividly in my mind, and we were concerned to the point where I was actually getting goosebumps.

It was incredibly freaky, and the principal eventually came out

---

Day 138: *We are not overweight because we eat a lot; we eat a lot because we are overweight #Obesity*
Day 139: *Make a random stranger's day special #SpecialDay*

with a bottle of black liquid, which was quite surprising. We had no idea what it was. He said nothing to us other than that we were safe to go back into the dormitory to sleep. Obviously, that whole evening most of us didn't sleep as we were in shock. It became laughable later on that night, where we even played Jinn jokes on each other. Yeah, boys will be boys! At this stage, I was still in disbelief that it was a Jinn. How could it possibly be?

We had morning classes before sunrise in which we would pass the institution's office on the way. That same bottle of black liquid was on the office windowsill, and it had turned into ash and as I read up more about it and after we had discussed it, I discovered that it was the ash of the Jinn, and it was a bad one. My disbelief had changed into a belief that it was in fact, a Jinn.

That was when I knew that I would not be going there for the second year. Jinns are usually present in places of religious knowledge or where people from monotheist faiths continuously attempt to get closer to the Almighty.

Although my mother wanted me to learn, safety for us children was always the priority. To this day, I don't know why I couldn't find the words to explain what was happening in the institution. I know that if I had spoken about my experiences, I would have been taken out immediately.

The thought of re-enrolling would not have even been a consideration! Although there was a number of hardships and challenges that year, it allowed me to become much stronger when I eventually returned home that same year. A number of challenges that I experienced during my high school and university years enabled me to be steadfast and embracing of challenges.

Cricket taught me the same thing: we can either duck, dive, defend the ball or hit it out the park! I either watched the ball

Day 140: Know who is in and out of your varied circles but try to get as many as possible in your immediate circle #LifeCircles
Day 141: Embrace criticism, it's not harmful, it helps you grow and learn #Criticism

closely, left it if it wasn't worthy to be hit or hit the ball when it was in the right place to do so. Obviously, the challenges during boarding school were not as devastating when compared to what others go through on a daily basis.

Being out of your comfort zone, allows you to not only be confident but to be stronger from both a spiritual and personal perspective; nothing would hinder the bark of someone's tree. Who knew that just ONE year at this institution would allow someone to grow so exponentially?

I keep questioning myself that if it were not for this year at boarding school, the experience of being in that environment (out of my comfort zone), would I be where I am today? I wonder, and God knows best. Thank you, Mom!

High School

Similarly to primary school, going to high school was either by foot, bus or catching lifts with friends. I could never forget Appa Salma Badat, and her daughters, Mumtaaz and Shameema, for lifting me to high school for three consecutive years. Words will never be able to explain how much I appreciated it! We also enjoyed listening to Darren "Whackhead" Simpson's prank calls on 94.7 Highveld Stereo every morning on the way to school. Today, I still have the privilege of listening to him on Kfm in the mornings.

I had schooled at Roosevelt High School in Roosevelt Park. I chose the following subjects as I knew that I wanted to help people by venturing into the health sciences by either doing Physiotherapy or Biokinetics: English, Afrikaans, Mathematics, Physical Science, Biology, Accounting and a seventh subject, Economics.

Day 142: Always put principles before passion #Principles
Day 143: Support your team, even when they don't perform well #TrueSupport

Going back home was always great, but on some days it was quiet and lonely. My sister and brother had relocated for work purposes, and I missed them a lot. My sister left St. Vincent's and moved to Australia to leverage her career. My brother went to Mpumalanga to do his community service. Through both these relocations, my brother and sister had met and married their soul mates.

We stayed in front of a park and quite often after going to the mosque which was after high school, I used to find a quiet space in the park to breathe, walk, think or play sport with members from the neighbourhood. I used to either visualise for the upcoming cricket match or unimaginably dream of where life would possibly take me.

At this age, everything was about cricket. The dream of playing for the Proteas was prominent. That was until one day during a school game for Roosevelt High School, during my gather in my bowling, something snapped in my lower back on the left-hand side. It was excruciatingly painful. It was so painful that even if I tripped over a brick or step with my left foot, it hurt a lot. It was a sort of pain that was felt with movements, but surprisingly not much with batting. It wasn't a dull ache pain but was a sharp, radiating pain at the bottom left of my back that would radiate towards the spine. Clinically, it was known as a spondylolysis, a stress fracture in the spine. Mine was on the third lumbar vertebra (L3).

I did not bowl fast again after that happened. I was supposed to go for under-19 trials but couldn't go. The dream of playing professional cricket was shattered. Despite the fact that I was the 1st team cricket captain (2006-2007) and later had a cricket scholarship to go study at the University of Johannesburg. This sadly wasn't enough.

Day 144: *Tipping shouldn't be a 10% norm; courtesy should be part of our moral code #Courtesy*
Day 145: *Pay attention to our children and love them #Children*

University

One of the biggest turning points in my life was when I had just completed matric. I had to choose between county cricket in the United Kingdom or studying a Bachelors in Sport Psychology at the University of Johannesburg. I am so grateful today that I chose UJ, and not the UK. I received a small bursary from UJ to play cricket for them. Many people in Johannesburg remember me as the walker.

Each day, I walked from home to university which took me about 45 minutes. I remember that one enduring road along the way, Mercury Road in Crosby. It was so good for fitness because of the uphill walk, but I always looked forward to coming back home because it was downhill. On Tuesdays to Thursdays it was cricket practice, so I had to walk with my 'coffin' (cricket bag).

It was heavy, but it was my form of training, carrying the bag alternating between my shoulders. I walked to university every day for two years, but perhaps that was a bad idea as I re-injured my lower back severely and couldn't play cricket for another six months. My first back injury happened in matric (2007), as mentioned earlier – this was when my dream of becoming a professional cricketer did not come true. If I were a biokineticist then and knew better, I would have tried an alternative plan. Subsequently, my bursary in my second and third year of university fell through.

During my three years at university, I was a cricket coach at Parkview Senior School. From UJ to Parkview was a 90-minute walk. I dreaded Tuesdays and Thursdays because that meant a total of 270 minutes of walking per day (135 minutes going and 135 minutes coming back; I couldn't afford to take a bus or taxi). I was earning R150 a day and coached two days a week. I was getting roughly R1,000 to R1,200 per month.

Day 146: Understand and listen to someone's struggles #Listen&Understand
Day 147: People are our greatest assets – treasure every single person that you have met along your life journey #GreatestAsset

That was enough for my meals, airtime and the odd coffee with friends. My parents were working-class people and could only afford the bare essentials at home. I am grateful till this day that they taught me gratitude, appreciation and did not spoil me. I don't regret a single moment, but a plan had to be made for my fees.

I was always a daredevil type of guy who wanted to try my hand at most things. I learned the concept of cricket coaching clinics when I saw something on television one day. I then started having cricket coaching clinics every holiday for children around Johannesburg. It was called the HN Cricket Coaching Academy.

I am grateful that I still use my HN (Habib Noorbhai) brand till today – humble beginnings. The academy was not just to make money and pay off items that I needed, but it also became so enjoyable.

Cricket coaching increased my love for children. There was one point when I conducted a clinic with no profit, and I didn't mind because I enjoyed working with the boys and helping them improve their game, but I couldn't be profitless for every clinic. I eventually made some profit and paid for my fees in my second and third year at UJ. Mr Feizal Kimmie, a cricket enthusiast and mentor, played an imperative role in my life during these early years and I will never forget him and his wife, Mrs Zara Kimmie.

The Airtel Champions League (2010)

Mr Kimmie informed me of the 2010 Champions League coming to South Africa and encouraged me to apply to work for one of the teams in the tournament. He also put in a good word for me.

I thankfully got in.

Day 148: Sometimes you have to look through a different lens to appreciate your blessings #Blessings

Day 149: Great leaders don't set out to be leaders, they set out to make a difference. It's never about the role – but always about the goal #Leadership

Although most would have hoped to work for the Mumbai Indians or Chennai Super Kings, I was assigned to the Redbacks from South Australia. They were the sleeping giants of the competition.

I got to know the guys really well. These cricketers, along with my brother-in-law, Abdel Karim, who is Australian, showed me that Australians are wonderful people – despite the bantering between South Africa and Australia for sporting occasions. They place a huge emphasis on family and caring for their loved ones. My sister and her family live there too, and they love it.

An embarrassing, yet funny moment, during the Champions League, was when I thought I had lost the former Aussie cricketer Shaun Tait's bag. I was in charge of team logistics and had to ensure that all the players' bags were transported safely, either via plane, bus or trucks. If a certain number of bags were uploaded, I had to be sure that the exact number got off. A simple task, you'd think.

No, it's not that simple when players taking the Mickey out of you. I had counted 67 bags that had left Johannesburg one day. We were going to play against the Mumbai Indians and Royal Challengers at the Kingsmead Stadium in Durban that week.

Upon arrival in Durban, the truck had taken off 67 pieces of luggage at the Elangeni Hotel, but I had only counted 66 in the hotel foyer. I never messed up in Jozi, and now I was panicking. After all the bags were sent to the players' rooms, Shaun came to me and asked: "Where's my bag, mate?"

"Taity, is it not in front of your hotel room or the hotel foyer?" I asked.

He said: "I checked both places and it's not there. My spikes were in that training bag."

Now I was extremely worried. How could their strike bowler not train or play against the Indian cricketing giants? He was an asset

Day 150: Awareness is admirable, but doing is better #Doing
Day 151: Maintain dignity with every person you encounter #HumanDignity

to the team. Like a headless chicken, I searched every floor in the hotel, all players' rooms, the foyer, truck, hotel gym and even the hotel kitchen.

The team manager summoned me to his room.

"Oh, snap!" I uttered.

My mate (and former team liaison manager), Niaz Ahmed, was there as well as the captain, manager and the big guy himself, Mr Shaun Tait. I expected the worst. Shaun then smiled and held the training bag in front of me saying it was all a joke.

Do you know that feeling when you are relieved, in shock, laughing and annoyed at the same time? I was just that. I just shook my head with a smile and walked out of the room. Wherever I went afterwards, Shaun was there and would laugh. We are good friends until today, and the little bag incident is what cemented our bond during the tournament. The players and managers had enjoyed my work ethic and my involvement, so they wanted to play a joke on me.

That's not all.

When we went back to SuperSport Park in Centurion, the Redbacks had prepared for their semi-final game against the Chevrolet Warriors. The Redbacks – yes, the sleeping giants – was the only team in the tournament to have not lost a group stage match. They had won all their group matches against the Highveld Lions, Mumbai Indians, Royal Challengers Bangalore and Guyana.

In Centurion, Shaun had asked me to throw him some balls because he wanted to bat a bit. Niaz was amped and came down with me. We jokingly asked Shaun: "If I bowl to you and get you out, what would I get?"

"If you get me out, I'll buy you a meal," he promised.

"If you get me out twice... Errrr... Uhmmm... You can have a night with Mashoom."

Day 152: Research, education and support are integral for the prevention and early detection of cancer #Cancer

Day 153: Walk | Run | Stand up for cancer #LaceUpForCancer

Mashoom (his girlfriend at the time, now turned wife) was a model back in India. I was excited, and said, "Game on!" Not that I would have taken him up on his second deal if I had got him out twice.

So here goes.

Bearing in mind that I was injured in 2007 and that I would not bowl fast again, I gave it my best shot. I got Shaun out. It was a genuine edge. Meal? Done! I was now pumped up and "wanting Mashoom."

I kept on bowling and Shaun had a decent defence which explained what kept him at the crease for a longer duration. Through my Ph.D. in cricket batting, I discovered that batsmen with a solid, good defence would be more likely to keep you longer at the crease even when you didn't score too many runs. I have come to realise today that he certainly had the potential to do so.

I then bowled. He edged the ball to the pole of the net (i.e. to gulley; a 45-degree angle to the batsman).

I proclaimed: "That's Mashoom!"

We all laughed.

"No, no mate," he said. "I said a genuine edge. Not any edge. A genuine edge. That wouldn't be out in a game." Until today, I grill him about that, but I have to respect him. After all, he's married now.

My time working with the South Australian team was undoubtedly the most amazing experience during my undergraduate years. I experienced the professional sports platform that included logistics, security, a high-level of professionalism and being competent in all areas of your duties. Of course, I also enjoyed the free lodging in expensive hotels with some of the best players, travelling with them, getting free food and subsistence (a daily allowance) for

---

Day 154: *Every step equates to a week and 52 weeks equates to a year #StepByStep*
Day 155: *Gain insights and understanding from the government to specifically understand what the gaps are and how to implement what's needed in your country #Understanding*

being involved with the team.

The Redbacks, unfortunately, lost the semi-final by 20 odd runs. The Chennai Super Kings subsequently went on to win the trophy at The Wanderers Stadium in Johannesburg.

Post-graduate Years

I wanted to become a biokineticist to help athletes with their rehabilitation because I knew what it took after being injured. However, knowing how it felt and studying it was two different things. Out of approximately 100 undergrads, universities were only accepting between 10 and 15 Honours students. The selections were tough.

I persevered, made the requirements and thankfully got accepted into UJ, UWC, Wits and UKZN. UKZN had ignited that passion for research and was my first choice. Why? I missed my brother a lot and wanted to spend time with him. I was also tired of Johannesburg and wanted a change of scenery. I eventually moved to Durban in 2011 where I completed my Honours in Biokinetics.

The year went by very quickly. I will never know how to thank my brother for all the support he gave me during that year, and even until today. He's a truly remarkable man. I honestly couldn't have asked for a better brother.

Day 156: Be a role model to the youth and all those around you #Role-Model
Day 157: Testicular cancer needs a lot more attention and awareness than it currently has #TesticularCancer

10
The Move to Cape Town

As mentioned earlier ("The Second Branch"), the last six years in the Mother City has been a journey of character and professional development. One of my highlights is my very own heart-driven emporium, The Humanitarians.

In my first year as a Capetonian, in 2012, I met two rocks who shared this journey with me, Taahira Moola and Noel Adams.

Taahira was and still is a student at UCT, and Noel was the manager of the varsity's Obz Square residence. Our non-profit organisation, The Humanitarians, would not have achieved much without these two amazing people. I treasure them a lot.

I have learned so much from them; not just about community engagement but about life itself. We are also each other's support structures. The projects and initiatives we conducted were novel and exciting, and amidst the challenges, we persevered. We had limitations as well, including exposure and funding for the NPO. This was one of the main reasons for entering Mr South Africa in 2015. We will talk more about The Humanitarians and Mr South Africa in the later chapters.

Travelling

The travel bug bit me between 2012 and 2017 while living in Cape Town. Thankfully, academia had given me the opportunity to do

---

Day 158: Devote your time towards the physically disabled #PhysicalDisabilities
Day 159: *Continue disseminating tolerance and harmony among all faiths and cultures; build bridges and not walls #BuildBridges*

so by attending many conferences, research seminars or meetings. Fortunately, I had travelled to all continents except to North America. When you travel, you begin to realise how small the world is, despite each nation's minute differences.

You grow. You become not only street-smart but a smart traveller.

My list of travels include:

2012: Sydney and Melbourne, Australia – Australian Sports Medicine Congress;

2013: Paris and Barcelona, Spain – European Congress of Sports Science;

2014: Rio de Janeiro, Brazil – International Congress of Physical Activity and Public Health;

2015: Sydney, Australia – World Congress of Science and Medicine in Cricket; Manchester and London, UK – Congress of Sports Science and Technology; Umrah (an Islamic pilgrimage) with my brother and father, a spiritual trip to Medina and Mecca; Chennai and Mumbai, India – Arthroscopy, Sports Science and Sports Medicine Conference;

2016: London, Edinburgh and Glasgow, UK – Research meetings and field work; and

2017: Goa, Jaipur, Agra and Delhi, India – Conference in Sports Science and meetings.

The move to Cape Town helped to develop me on both professional and personal levels. It was during this time, in 2013, where I was also part of the Top 100 Brightest Young Minds (BYM) in South Africa.

BYM is a youth development programme that identifies promising and up-and-coming individuals between the ages of 18 and 33, by application and selection. This was a formidable experience

Day 160: Encourage more women and girls to enter into the fields of science # WomenScience
Day 161: Pay respect and gratitude to those working in radio #Radio

where we – as a group of "bananas" (the colloquial term used by BYM for "bright minds") could share the same platform, exchange ideas, deliberate, learn and engage on an array of topics.

It was through this summit that I got to meet the late politician, political prisoner, and anti-apartheid activist Ahmed Kathrada. I will never forget what he told me. When I shook his hand, he looked me straight in the eye and said: "It's all in your (the youth's) hands now".

Since then, I made it a promise to him, myself and to the South African people, to carry on the great work that he, Madiba and other freedom fighters such as Oliver Tambo and Walter Sisulu had started. The essence of continuity is key for any great start.

Two years later, I was also nominated as one of the *Mail and Guardian's* Top 200 Young South Africans for 2015. Again, this was another platform where young minds were able to engage, learn and share with one another. This nomination was encouraging, and through this experience, I also got to meet a former mayor of Gauteng and other notable dignitaries.

Travelling and specifically, long-distance driving had always been a hobby of mine. During 2016, I conducted a 40-day research road trip around the country. The objective was to collect as much data as possible from our nation's semi-professional and professional cricketers. The result was that I was able to test and work with 155 South African cricketers from all nine provinces and drove 8 030 kilometres.

However, the trip was not only for research purposes. I also had some hours during the day to explore our beautiful country – alone. From this experience, it reassured me that South Africa is such a beautiful country to live in, despite its challenges. Any country has their challenges, so why move anywhere else?

Day 162: *I'm a believer of continuous love and that we should love each other every day #UnconditionalLove*

Day 163: *Sometimes we must look through a child's eyes and work towards a different, better world #WorldPeace*

You will not find any other country like South Africa that boasts beautiful terrains, oceans, wonderful people (with a great sense of humour!), cultural diversity, 11 official languages, and many other heritages that we can be proud of.

On such trips, when driving for such a long time by your lonesome self, you get to reflect quite a bit. You ponder how far you've come and how much further you still have to go in life. Touché, at this point, I had only driven 1,000 kilometres and still had another 7,000 odd kilometres to go.

I also witnessed the serious poverty that exists, especially in the Eastern Cape, KwaZulu-Natal, Mpumalanga and Limpopo. We have a lot to be grateful for, every day. Counting our blessings on a daily basis, therefore, is fundamental to maintaining our life's purpose and finding our happiness. This observation provided me with the re-affirmation, that by entering Mr South Africa, it would allow me to do much more for our country, as best as I could, whether I won or not.

Returning to Cape Town after the road trip in 2016 had ended, allowed me to start just that, amidst my priorities at work and completing my Ph.D.

The reasons for sharing my experiences on BYM, MG Top 200 YSA, being part of Fast Company's Top 30 creative business people in South Africa, and travelling, is to inspire others, especially the youth. You can achieve anything you set your mind to do.

I was criticised a lot growing up and throughout my career.

Through each of these doubts in my abilities there were many painful experiences, but then there was subsequent pleasure in proving them wrong. That's what you simply have to do. However, don't do it to prove them wrong or show what you are truly capable of, but do it because you have a realistic and adequate sense of

---

Day 164: Spend time with special needs kids and support them #SpecialNeedsKids
Day 165: Uplift and inspire the youth to be more than they can envision #UpliftYouth
Day 166: When life throws you obstacles, throw it back harder or hit it for six #LifeObstacles

belief within yourself and know your true worth.

Living in four cities around South Africa (Johannesburg, Pretoria, Durban and Cape Town) and making the 40-day road trip around the country, certainly also shaped the person that I have become. It has allowed me to experience and become well versed with the diversity of our culture and an array of personnel. It gave me the opportunity to communicate and interact with a wide range of people and helped me to learn about their hard yards too.

What's the point of it all, you might ask.

With these experiences, I can provide my two cents worth of advice, especially to the youth:

- Take the initiative and be proactive. Never wait for something to happen. You need to know when to be patient for certain things and when to persist for others.
- Spend most of your time outside of your comfort zone to become resilient.
- Community work done with sincerity will open a number of doors for you without you even noticing. It creates the sense of fulfilment and calming effect within because you have witnessed a transformation in someone's life because of your acts of good or kindness.
- When you try and force a door open, it will remain shut. Give it time.
- Work smart. Not hard. Be patient, have a vision and trust the process.
- Expose yourself to as much as possible to open your eyes to the world (studying, travelling, relationships, learning and the crucial values of etiquette).

Day 167: Don't let the success of others be your failure #Success&Failure
Day 168: *A week can't take off without an efficient, planned runway #PlanYourRunway*
Day 169: *Be proud of your mother tongue and share it with others #MotherTongue*

- Make minor mistakes; learn from them but don't repeat those mistakes.
- Criticism is your greatest motivational tool; not to prove others wrong, but to become stronger, in deciding which things to switch on and switch off from.
- Be authentic, be the best version of yourself. Continuously "upgrade" yourself.
- Be good to everybody who crosses your life path. But keep few, quality friends.
- Love always. Live with purpose. Laugh sufficiently and make a difference.

Day 170: *Referrals are not just professional, they are courtesy #Referrals*
Day 171: *Support a foundation that empowers people to live healthier #SupportFoundations*
Day 172: *Never forget your footprints – they are the shaft of your life bone #Footprint*

11
My Perspectives on Leadership

If you ask me what makes a very good leader, I will probably tell you that it is about leading by example, but we all know that there is much more to it than just that. The father of South Africa's nation, Former President Nelson Mandela, played a pivotal role at being a leader in our country.

He once said: "When a man has done what he considers to be his duty to his people and his country he can rest in peace. I believe that I have done that and made every effort and that is, therefore, why I will sleep for the eternity."

Madiba is known around the globe as one of the greatest leaders of all time.

There are more than 400,000 results of leadership definitions you could explore on the internet or in the dictionary. These will highlight a variety of aspects of what leadership actually is. The aim of this chapter is to show you how you can develop into becoming a true leader going forward – and learning from various types of leadership perspectives.

There are also a variety of literature sources that can show you the different types of leadership styles that can be employed and the books can inculcate and educate you on the most valuable principles and values of a leader. I would like to take you through my

Day 173: Support, raise funds for cancer and remove the stigma that it kills #CancerStigma
Day 174: *Support fundraisers that contribute towards great causes #SupportFundraisers*
Day 175: *Be someone ordinary who does extraordinary things #Extraordinary*

personal inspirers and mentors who have guided me throughout my career as a young leader. Perhaps, these will add value to you too.

Firstly, I'd like to mention the American business magnate Bill Gates. In his book, *With the road ahead,* he says that "the thinkers rule the workers" and therefore in this modern era, especially through innovation, we need to start working smart. We need to think very differently compared to the others.

Secondly, our very own Madiba through his book *Long Walk to Freedom* says: "Lead from the back, make everyone think that they are actually in the front." That is why he was one of the most diplomatic leaders the world has ever known, which aspired him to be remarkable in front of the world especially during the Apartheid era in South Africa.

The American statesman and lawyer Abraham Lincoln said: "Nearly all people can overcome adversity but if you want to test a man's character give him power and you will see the type of leader that he can be."

The American civil rights leader Dr Martin Luther King Jr, who died at the tender age of 39, played an instrumental role in the lives of young Americans during the struggle in the late 1970s. He inspired the virtues of hope, vision and dreams. He said: "A person's life begins to an end when he forgets all the matters in life that mean the most," and that is the key message he left behind.

Mahatma Gandhi, the leader of the Indian independence movement, through his inspirational roles during the British East India Company in India and then coming to South Africa, said: "Be the change that you what to see in the world."

We feel that leaders are all about muscles at the time. Right now, we know that it is much more than that. It is about being a people's person.

Day 176: Motivate the youth on how to adopt life stamina in all facets of their lives #LifeStamina
Day 177: New month, new moon, new challenges, challenge yourself #ChallengeYourself

George Washington, who was known as America's most indispensable man during the American Revolution, said something simple: "Leadership is about being an example, and you can see from a leader whether he will be good or bad."

Sir Alex Ferguson, through his run with Manchester United Football Club for 26 years, said in his autobiography: "You are as good as your last match." Similarly, in an academic sector, you are as good as your last exam; you are as good as your last meeting in the corporate world. That is the kind of principle Ferguson established with his team for many years.

Steve Waugh was the only test cricket captain to have a test-win ratio of 71%, and in his autobiography, *Out of my comfort zone*, he showed that he always played out of his comfort zone. He was one of the best sporting captains who had a temperament that no other could touch.

Furthermore, I would like to comment on Professor Tim Noakes who I am privileged to have had as my Ph.D. supervisor. He has been, still is and always will be an inspiration to me as a scientist and researcher. Through his memoir, *Challenging Beliefs*, he said something to me: "If you plan to do something, you need to have the arrogance to do it, but when doing it, you need to have humility when conducting it."

That is why, to me, he will be known as one of the greatest scientists and researchers the world has ever seen.

Lastly, through the book *The Art of War* by Sun Tzu, the virtues and values that have been instilled in me are very enlightening. It has taught me that the greatest combats are won with diplomacy and humility, not violence or vindication.

I am going to take you through my personal leadership experiences; fortunately, I have had the opportunity to take on various

---

Day 178: Materialism should never take precedence over character or social responsibility #Materialism
Day 179: Are you prepared for JASON? (July, August, September, October, November) #JASON

leadership roles at UJ, UKZN and UCT. However, it started at a much younger age.

In 2006 and 2007 I was the first team's cricket captain. In 2009 and 2010, I was the chairperson of the Muslim Students' Association in which we played an integral role with the Student Representative Council at UJ. On that aspect, I was even awarded best chairperson for the Student Society.

In 2012 and 2013, I was fortunate to be the academic head at the FIT Principles Academy. In 2013, I was a third-tier sub-warden at Obz Square and later, was also the chairperson of the newly formed senior residence development council (now known as the Residence Academic Development Council). Since 2013, I am also the director and founder of The Humanitarians with an exceptional team of humanitarians and volunteers. All of these experiences have helped me grow exponentially in the sport, cultural, humanitarian, academic and social settings.

From my experience, I always questioned what principles actually govern successful leadership. The three principles that really stood out for me were: being passionate about what you are doing, being a people's person and having a high emotional intelligence. Those core principles have taught me not only to be a steadfast individual but also to be a successful leader.

How have these roles had a positive impact not only on myself as a leader but on the teams I have worked with? Firstly, it is about changing people's lives. There is no better feeling than actually going out there and changing the lives of others. Ask yourself right now, are you conducting humanitarian work or voluntary work right in your current time span? The current challenge we have in South Africa is that the youth and young leaders are not taking the initiative to take up leadership roles, whether it is a humanitarian or

---

Day 180: Educate and inspire healthy families #InspireHealthily
Day 181: True bonding is not measured by the time spent together or the favours done for each other #bonding

academic perspective, or even within a sporting or cultural setting.

This is what we currently need to do. We need to have a shift in our mindset. Madiba taught us that our nation has a turbulent history. We need to continue being an inspiration to others and not to stop. It needs to diversify and continue. It is about getting out of your comfort zone and seeing where the magic happens.

If I may comment again on the time of the Apartheid struggle with Nelson Mandela and his Rivonia trialists. They had advised Mandela that it was admirable what he wanted to do and achieve for the nation and its people but he needed to remember that if he wanted to make a substantial change and difference, he needed to work together with them. By working together, we are better than one and will be able to go far. It is not effective leadership without admirable teamwork. That is the kind of virtues that they had portrayed.

Let's think differently again. I want to paint a picture in your mind.

If you have a stem of authority and if you are a leader, you can either be one of two things. You can either be a follower where you lead any person big or small, old or young or you can be the sheep or the shepherd where you are part of the flock or the shepherd that leads the flock. Do you want to be the person that is following other sheep or the shepherd that is leading the sheep?

In addition, you can either be a part of the wolf pack where you are leading the pack or are a part of the pack that is driving forward. From a different perspective, you can lead by example, and importantly, in many sectors not only in South Africa but abroad – leaders need to get off their high horses. This is because only when we see ourselves on the ground and off our high horses, that is, again, where the magic happens.

Day 182: The same boiling water that softens potatoes, hardens eggs #Circumstance
Day 183: Humanitarianism is a way of life #Humanitarianism

In this era, we need to be innovative, creative and instead of asking questions like "how" or "when", we should rather be asking questions like "why" and "what if". Through asking those questions, we can establish that it is not about making things right but instead, doing the right things.

When we do that, we can identify ourselves as different positions on the chessboard, whether as a pawn, knight, bishop, castle, a queen or king. From then, when we see ourselves on the chessboard, we can take ourselves and move forward, execute and lead effectively.

Day 184: *Educate and mentor students sustainably so that the next year of students can be inspired by them #SustainableTeaching*

Day 185: *Teach teachers how to coach and teach their learners #TeachTheTeachers*

Sitting at home at the tender age of 1, 1989.

On Market Street, age 5, 1993, in Johannesburg, where my mom and sister took a picture of me. I look sad because I thought they were going to leave me.

Coming back from Badplaas where I went for an excursion with school friends, age 14, 2003.

The privilege of working with the South Australian Redbacks during the Airtel Champions League T20 tournament, staged in South Africa. This was taken at the Wanderers cricket stadium in Johannesburg, age 21, 2010.

One of the first moments after moving to Cape Town, Table Mountain, age 23, 2012.

The amazing tripod of The Humanitarians: Noel Adams, Taahira Moola and myself, age 23, 2012.

Having a sacred moment with a kangaroo in Melbourne, Australia, age 23, 2012. This was after attending the Australian Sports Medicine Congress in Sydney.

A trip to Paris (above) before attending the European Congress of Sports Science in Barcelona (below). This was taken place at Gaudi's sculpture. Age 24, 2013.

Overlooking the sugar loaf mountain and at the tip of Christ Redeemer in Rio de Janiero, Brazil. Attending the International Congress of Physical Activity and Public Health. Age 25, 2014.

The privilege of visiting Old Trafford in Manchester, while on a research trip in the United Kingdom. Age 26, 2015.

Meeting the late Ahmed Kathrada at the final evening of South Africa's Brightest Young Minds Summit at Moyo, Zoo Lake, Johannesburg. Age 24, 2013.

With the mayor of Gauteng after being nominated in Mail and Guardians Top 200 Young South Africans. Age 26, 2015.

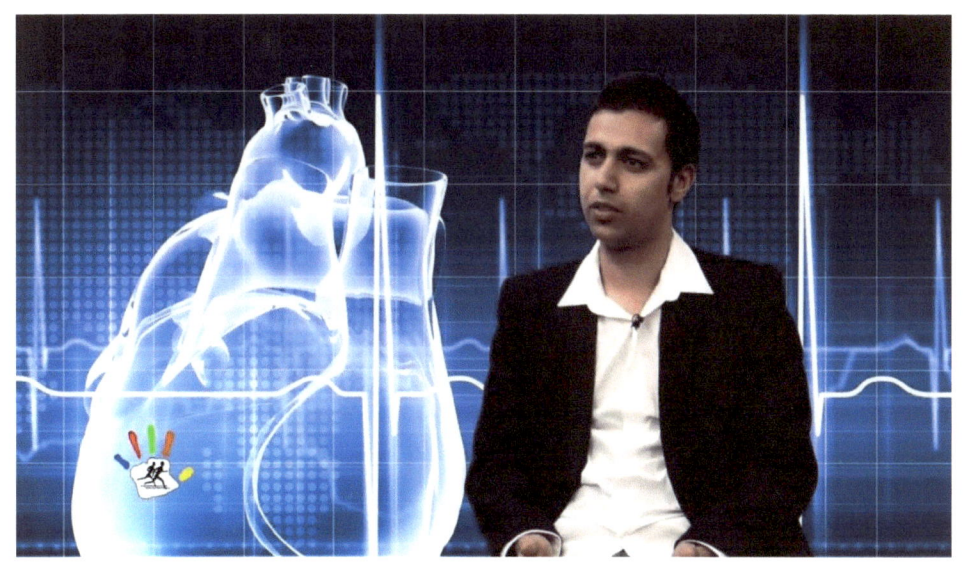

Presenting my own sport and health show on OpenView HD. Age 26, 2015.

Meeting Prof. Tim Noakes for some advice before flying out to Syndey again, this time, for the World Congress of Science and Medicine in Cricket. Age 26, 2015.

Myself and Russell Woolmer doing the honours of inaugurating our coaching cricket bat into the Lords Cricket Museum in London. An innovative tool that had emanated from my PhD in cricket batting. Age 27, May 2016.

Graduation photos of my Bachelors (2011), Honours (2012), Masters (2014) and Doctoral (2017). Note: same shirt. Consistency is everything. I treasured every moment in my 10 years of varsity.

Getting capped by the Vice-Chancellor and Registrar of UCT for my PhD in the same year of my Mr South Africa reign. I couldn't have asked for two better blessings in one year. July 2017, Age 28.

Former Mr SA (1996) – Dr. Michael Mol. Current Mr SA (2017) – Dr. Habib Noorbhai. The only two Mr South Africa's with Doctor's titles since 1982. May 2017.

Welcoming my family (the amazing 5 together in one place) at the Cape Town International Airport – a priceless picture and one of the happiest moments in my life. End of 2016.

Visiting the Taj Mahal in Agra, India. January 2017. After my research visit in Jaipur and Delhi, with a keynote address at the International Congress of Sports Science and Physical Education.

Being the Master of Ceremonies at the Youth event at the Cape Sun: Orange the World. Speaking to in front of 400 youth delegates. End of 2016.

Meeting with Democratic leader, Mmusi Maimane, at Parliament. January 2017.

Meeting with Deputy President of South Africa, Cyril Ramaphosa at the Western Cape Chamber of Commerce. February 2017.

The wonderful students that I lectured at the Cape Peninsula University of Technology. Picture taken after our community engagement project. May 2017.

Shaking hands with CANSA Corporate Relations Manager, Munnik Marais, after raising R10,000 for CANSA and more than R1 million in exposure after driving 5000km around South Africa to create exposure and spread awareness for cancer. April 2017.

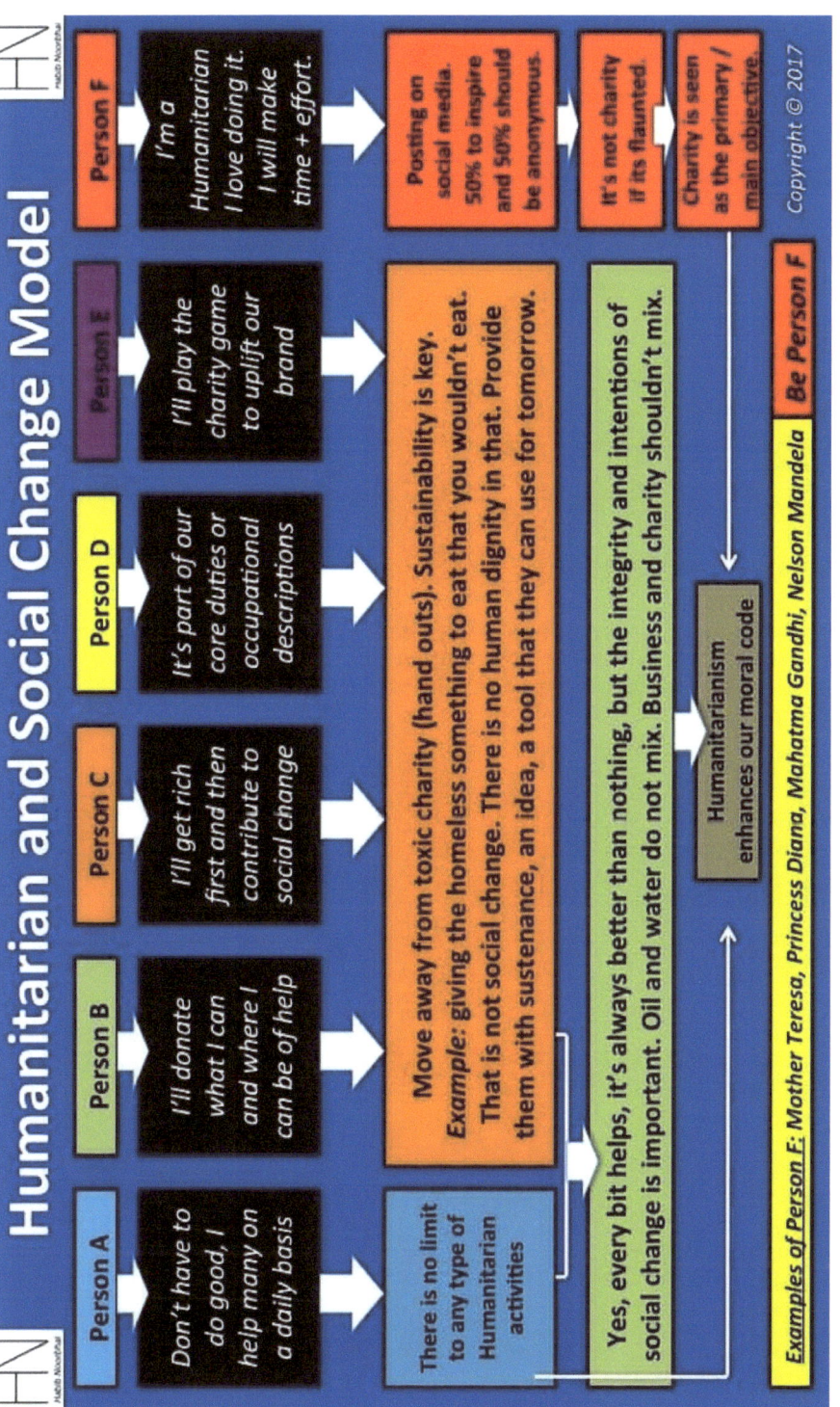

The Humanitarian and Social Change Model that I have created, which can be replicated to an array of sectors and target the challenges that we face in society.

Educating community members of Manengberg on how to sustain themselves during the month of Ramadaan using their sustainable hamper. We fed over 100 families prior to the month of Ramadaan. May 2017.

Educating members in Mitchell's Plain how to adopt a sustainable lifestyle through healthy and affordable means. March 2017.

A newspaper article published in The Plain on the community projects done as Mr South Africa. April 2017.

A newspaper article published in The Rising Sun on how I have used my Mr SA title to break stereotypes and placing an emphasis of brawn over beauty.

Mr SA changes the face of pageants

ATHINA MAY

When you think of Mr South Africa, you may envision a muscular figure who distracts you with his charm and visual appeal, and although the current Mr SA does this, he managed to take the crown without taking his shirt off.

Observatory's Habib Noorbhai, 29, who recently graduated with a PhD in exercise science at UCT, is also the first Muslim man to win the pageant. He walked off with the title in November last year.

Mr Noorbhai entered Mr SA to draw attention to his non-profit organisation, The Humanitarians, which he founded in 2013. The volunteer-based organisation, promotes a healthy lifestyle, skills training, education and sport development.

Mr Noorbhai is also a sport science lecturer at the Cape Peninsula University of Technology (CPUT) and he hopes to use his position as a biokineticist and researcher to create change in South African communities. He entered the pageant with encouragement from his friends, but not without his own reservations. "There were concerns that the Mr SA title would have negative implications such as sex appeal, modelling, alcohol brands, etc. But I always stuck to my morals and values. Fortunately, being authentic and being myself worked in my favour. I am the first Mr SA to have never taken off my clothes. I am the shortest and probably skinniest Mr SA in history."

He said his role as Mr SA had not been easy as he had had to balance his duties along with completing his PhD and running his NPO. But now that he has gradu-

■ Mr South Africa 2017, Observatory resident Dr Habib Noorbhai, recently graduated with a PhD in Exercise Science at the University of Cape Town.

■ Mr South Africa 2017 Habib Noorbhai, completed his PhD focused on the batting backlift technique in cricket.

ated, he plans to focus on assisting the poor this winter and working on a project with Nal'ibali, which found a rhythm for the remainder run reading clubs and other reading-for-enjoyment activities in communities across the country.

"It has been a tough year but it's been a journey of growth and strength. I am fortunate to have time out of their comfort zones of my reign and have embraced how to cope while often being in the public eye," he said.

His advice to youth wanting to follow in his footsteps is to work smart and be prepared.

To find out more about Noorbhai and the work he does, visit his website at http://habibnoorbhai.com

A newspaper article published in The Tatler Southern Suburbs, Cape Town, on how I have changed the face of pageants, thus inspiring the youth to start from the heart and not with beauty.

12
Heart

There are a variety of leaders, people and organisations that do formidable work and try to make a difference out there. The reality is that we can all define the words "humanitarian" or "philanthropist" in different ways. I would like to elaborate and discuss the true meaning of being a humanitarian.

To this end I would like to quote a passage from the Bible. Matthew 6:3 states: "When you give to someone in need, don't let your left hand know what your right hand is doing." That is ultimately what is so important to consider when helping or giving – that whatever you give to someone or when helping them from your heart, you must try your best to not remember it or let your left hand or your mind calculate what you have done for that person – in other words too, there must be nothing expected in return.

If you have to search for the word "humanitarian" on the internet, you will come up with more than 63,000 results showing you how a humanitarian can be defined. In my experience, I have summarised about 12 important values that can define a humanitarian.

These are a range of values from being a teacher, taking the initiative, doing community work through engagement, being committed to what you do, being punctual, enjoying what you are doing, loving what you do, coping with pressure, being organised at what you do, being passionate about what you are doing, having the drive to carry on with initiatives and being proactive in everything that you

---

Day 186: *Show your support towards kidney patients and the prevention of kidney disease #KidneyHealth*
Day 187: *Have few but quality friendships – value them #QualityFriendships*

do in the community or society. There are also other values that one can point out.

The three values that I consider the most important as a humanitarian are passion, drive and proactivity. When we do community work with our volunteers or through different organisations, I always try to inspire them to put on their "PDP caps". Not a "professional driving permit" but for them to be a passionate, driven and proactive individual when they go into the community.

Verily, you are going out of your comfort zone and most of the time you enter a community that you are not comfortable with or used to. It is something that you need to be passionate about, driven to do what you need to do and take proactive leadership without anyone telling you what to do.

The reasons why the above values are so important are because there are a variety of challenges that we see around the world, and not just in South Africa. These can range from public health to education, sustainability, the way we live in this modern age and the economy.

I would like to use an analogy.

If we could reduce the world to a village of 100 people with all existing human ratios remaining the same, what would the demographics look like?

About 60% would be Asians, more than 10% would be Europeans, approximately 5% would be US Americans and Canadians, under 10% Latin Americans and under 15% Africans – of that 51% would be male, 49% female, and 80% would have a dark skin colour and 20% would have a lighter complexion. Furthermore, about 80% would be living in sub-standard housing. More than 20% would not have any electricity and of the 75% that do have it, most would only use it for light at night.

Day 188: *Things can always be worse #CountYourBlessings*
Day 189: *Be humble in your confidence yet courageous in your character #Confidence*

Approximately 70% would not be able to read. Only one out of 100 would have a college education, and 50% would be malnourished, 1% dying of starvation, a third would be without access to safe water supply, 1% HIV positive, 1% near death, 2% near birth and 7% would have access to the internet.

These statistics are probably changing and evolving with a lot of change agents and social entrepreneurs trying to improve such challenges worldwide. The fundamental question is: how do we combat so many of the world's challenges with these concerning statistics? One of the many interventions that are out there is definitely humanitarianism. The message that I try to convey on a daily basis is that being a humanitarian is so important, even if it is just for five minutes. We all want to change the world. But we need to try our best to make a difference even if it's through one random act of kindness or helping people in that very moment. Collectively, if we all behave in this manner, we will slowly see the world shaping in a much better way.

I get to lecture quite a number of students so let's look at it from a student's perspective. When you look at the timetable of a typical learner's programme or his/her life priorities, you will notice that the timetable is quite busy but it varies during the week.

Within their programme, despite what they are studying, where they are working, or what they are doing; they probably have to fit up to 12 priorities within their lives. I have come up with about 12 priorities that students or the youth will consider to be important in their lives but they would only actually be able to fit some of these into their lives.

These range from family and friends, relationships, having a spiritual or religious/cultural connection, occupation, education, their children, social media, physical exercise, forms of entertainment,

---

Day 190: *"Reality is merely an illusion, albeit a very persistent one" – Albert Einstein #Illusion*
Day 191: *Building a digital world that consumers can trust is imperative #ConsumerRights*
Day 192: *Standing time is better than sitting time #StandAndWork*

eating, sleeping and reading. Those are probably the most common student priorities. The message here is that students need to think about how to integrate these priorities in order to achieve their desired goal and how they can accommodate humanitarian activities.

I always tell my students that if you are juggling a number of balls, if one ball drops, the chances are that all the balls will drop. What you want to try and do is to integrate your priorities, regardless of the number of them you have, so that you have a common purpose, a focal point or goal and things don't look all messy and end up in a juggling space.

So, what I did growing up and certainly when I entered the first year of university, was integrate all my priorities so that I could at least try and serve the community. That was my definitive purpose (being in service of others).

Of these, family, relationships, my religious duties and friendships were integral. These are what kept me sane, grounded and able to move forward. With that, I knew that my occupation, learning and diversifying my skills were important. I also acknowledged that a form of exercise was going to make me healthier and stronger, allowing me to do more.

By doing more, I sacrificed on entertainment. I had a few quality, good friends, and I also read from time to time. I integrated my priorities through coaching sport and community projects as a student on campus. The message here is: how do the youth integrate their priorities for a common purpose whether it is about having their own businesses, studying at college or university, trying to make a difference or trying to be successful irrespective of what their goals are?

At the end of the day, whatever you do, you have to differentiate

---

Day 193: *"Educating the mind without educating the heart is no education at all"*
– Aristotle #EducateTheHeart

Day 194: *Remember and appreciate legends #RememberLegends*

between what is ordinary and extraordinary and the difference is in the word "extra". The little extra you put in accounts for a categorical difference of 10% in whatever you do.

For example, if you are studying for an exam, you want to make sure that you give an additional 10%, because of that additional 10 minutes, an hour, whatever you can, try and add that 10% difference wherever you can, as that will be the difference between ordinary and extraordinary. The origin of "extra" is from the heart.

If you do anything because your heart is there, your mind and body will follow. If your heart is not there when doing it, your mind and body will be there by force, thereby not giving your full capability. The bottom-line is: do something that you will enjoy and add light to your heart!

A fundamental question that I am always asked by the youth is whether money should be at the centre of our attention. Key aspects such as family, relationships, work and education, materialism and spirituality, will always surround our centre of attention. The problem with that is that we are so focused on making money and earning a living, that sometimes the special people in our lives and those who are around us, can get neglected.

We should never let go of those who always held our hands.

The probable reason for why I think I am somewhat successful in my career is that I reversed that model. Instead of my focus and attention on the money, it went instead towards making a difference. Money was not the centre of my attention, but rather heart was the focus and putting my heart there for others allowed me to still manage my time with loved ones, relationships with friends, work, as well as education and spirituality.

Fortunately, I was never the type of guy with an emphasis on materialism until recently being crowned as Mr South Africa where I

Day 195: Make every day a Mandela day #MandelaDay
Day 196: Without hardships, we would not value ease #Hardships

want to look the part or be present at a number of events. Naturally, by having a heart and managing the priorities around you, work will maintain your living costs, and through other means, you will be able to try and make money here and there.

If you are a spiritual person you would know that ultimately money and wealth comes from God; the more you chase after wealth, the less time you spend with God. As a strong believer in God, the more attention you put towards God and still work hard on the side, God will hold your hand, and it is always about reaching out to God.

When you do this, you will be able to make a lot more of a difference, and you will question where you are getting this strength, energy and power from to do so much in such a short space of time? It is because you are putting trust in God and that is when God helps you.

The person who said it best was the Jamaican singer and songwriter Bob Marley. He said: "Some people are so poor that all they have is money." Therefore, richness is not defined by how much money you have but rather by your actions and heart.

This is why I would like to introduce you to the Humanitarian and Social Change Model (see picture attached in picture section). It discusses six different types of people within the Humanitarian community sector. My recommendation is that you want to try and be Person F as best as you can because charity is seen as a primary or main objective for this type of person, irrespective of the person's circumstances.

For such people, it is not charity if it is flaunted. Fifty percent of their Humanitarian work is anonymous and the other 50% they post on social media to inspire others. This is something that I tried to do during my reign as Mr South Africa, such as my 365 Heart

---

Day 197: *Stand up for your rights but practise your rights with responsibility #ResponsibleRights*

Day 198: *Reduce and reuse waste water #WasteWater*

campaign to mainly inspire and not to flaunt.

A lot of the charity activities that I carried out especially towards the latter part of my reign were not shown on social media. It comes back to the first quote: "Your left hand should not know what your right hand has done."

In essence, humanitarianism enhances our moral code irrespective of what our circumstances are and what our ages may be. My recommendation is to try to be Person F.

The other question we pose when going out into the community is: What kind of an egg are you?

As you know, an egg can be made in different ways: sunny-side up, scrambled, boiled, poached or even eaten raw and that indirectly speaks about the person that you can be when you are in the community. If you crack an egg, both the shell and the inside will spill. If you boil an egg, the only thing that breaks is the outside shell, and the inside stays intact.

This analogy shows that if your insides, your heart, is strong, no matter what happens on the outside, you will still be able to do community work and succeed. The root for humanitarian work starts with your heart; it cultivates the mind to do more, and when it does this it alleviates the soul. When this happens, your physical being becomes empowered, and in all four segments, you then become one complete passionate being in order to drive forward. That human who drives forward with his/her PDP is known as a true humanitarian.

Another question that you can pose is: What object are you in the community? Using these analogies can help especially in workshops. Are you a microwave that likes to get things done quickly? Or as an oven, do you like things to get done qualitatively through a process which takes time so that the outcome is better?

Day 199: Understand clouds and all things meteorological #Meteorological
Day 200: Spread awareness and support for Tuberculosis Day #EndTB
Day 201: Remember the victims of slavery #RememberSlavery

Do you like to be an iron with things straightened out? Or a tumble dryer where things are always going in circles to dry everything out? There are a number of analogies or objects that you can think about when doing work in the community.

With the same analogy, you can ask yourself what kind of animal you are in the community. Everyone wants to be a part of the cat family, a tiger, lion, but each animal has its own qualities. A good analogy for me was when I heard one of my students say that he was a chameleon and when asked why he said that, he said that chameleons are adaptable and are versatile in different situations.

The chameleon may not be your favourite animal or very common but it is an intriguing one. I have even heard people say they would like to be a mouse where they would like to curl up in a ball with others not catching or seeing them and run into their hole.

People also want to be an owl because very seldom will people notice them. They try to not be in the limelight but do what they can, yet they can still see everything around them from the top (an owl can rotate its head 365 degrees).

There are a number of animals that you can assimilate with; you just need to identify which one you are personally and which one suits you when you adapt in the community. There is no wrong or right egg, animal or object. It all depends on you as a person. Irrespective of what you choose, it is important to know which one you are and when you identify it, it can assist you to achieve the purpose of your living and truth. When you do that, you will then be able to apply yourself as a humanitarian in an array of situations.

The main humanitarian lesson that I have learnt is that there is an irony of age. As a child, we have energy and time but no money; as an adult, most have energy and money but limited time; and as an elderly person, most have money and time but limited energy.

Day 202: *Knowing what you want is one of the hardest things in life #KnowWhatYouWant*
Day 203: *Always strive to be the better version of yourself #BestVersionOfYourself*

So the irony of age is that throughout the span of life you only have one or two out of the three or nothing.

If you have all three at least at one stage of your life, then consider yourself privileged as the majority of the people in the community dream their whole lives about even having one out of three. They don't even have energy, time or money during their childhood as they are maybe malnourished.

As adults, they don't have all three as well but they may have time to make money to give them energy, and as elderly people, they may not even have money, energy or time due to poverty.

To the youth out there especially, you need to think very carefully where you are right now so that you can invest in your future down the line so that energy, time and money can be balanced throughout your life. Your time is everything, and that is the greatest asset (along with your health) that you can invest in, and not things in gold or silver (materialistic items).

The other lessons that I have learnt are that you want to be taking the initiative; you want to have proactive leadership, doing the right things without being told. You don't want to wait for your mom or dad, your guardian, god-parents or elder siblings to tell you to do it. You want to do it without being told.

As you mature, know what needs to be done. A true indicator of maturity is doing things without being told. The same applies to work in the community. When you identify a gap where you can take charge without someone telling you what to do, that makes you a proactive humanitarian and leader.

Even in your job, you can take proactive leadership but no matter what job you may have, remember that your job gives you authority, but your behaviour gives you respect. These values and virtues are everything and will create an everlasting impression with whichever

---

Day 204: *"When one door closes, another opens, but we often look so long and so regretfully upon the closed door that we do not see the one which has opened for us"*
– Alexander Graham Bell #ClosedDoors

Day 205: *Treasure and appreciate your freedom, don't abuse it #AppreciateYourFreedom*

organisation you work with. I would like you to picture a scenario where a lot of people have told you that the sky might be the limit. I would like to say that the sky might be the limit but know your limits through every cloud.

With every priority (cloud) that you have, you have to know and understand the limits of where you can go. The actor Bruce Lee said it the best and summed up my drive and career: "If you put limits in everything that you do, it will spread into your life and into your work, there are no limits, there are only plateaus, and you must not stay there, you must go beyond."

Lee said that there are no limits. There are only plateaus. Verily, you must know your limits depending on what your priorities are. When you know this, that priority is like a cloud because when you know your limits through every cloud, you will be able to penetrate this cloud, reach for a plateau state and subsequently understand what success is.

Success involves diligence, respect, responsibility, organisation, patience and planning and that acronym is so important (DRROP). The only time you will be successful is when you take that DRROP from that plateau/sky and when you do, not many people that are successful come down to earth.

Even if they are down to earth, they have two paths to choose from, where they can carry on and do their own thing and people might remember them, or they can help people and be a humanitarian and people will treasure them. Irrespective of which path they may take, they need to remember that people will criticise and underestimate their potential. It is their responsibility to prove them wrong, and in this role, they can show them what they are capable of.

Along with this road of criticism, remember that hardship

Day 206: *Collaborate with like-minded people to make a difference #Collaborate*
Day 207: *Prepare and mentor students for their examinations #ExamMentoring*

is designed to make you stronger, not weaker. An easy task or a quick fix is designed to make you weaker, not stronger; my advice is never taking the easy way out. Any hardship that you are facing is definitely going to make you stronger; the common saying is 'that which doesn't kill you makes you stronger'.

Irrespective of which organisation you work with and especially with regards to humanitarian initiatives, you will find in discussions quite often that you have contrasting views and differ from each other but remember that you may be "enemies in debate, but compatriots in action".

The only reason you are having that debate, and are enemies then, is because you are all working towards the same goal or path of trying to make a difference and that already makes you compatriots in action or in any struggle you are working towards. Whatever action you are striving towards, remember that correct action starts with correct thinking and correct thinking starts with the correct mindset, and only with a correct mindset, will you be able to understand the true meaning of being a humanitarian and take action.

Talking about action, I would like to discuss an initiative that is so close to my heart and which I believe is key to solving challenges not only in South Africa but around the world. This initiative is called the One-Person-Initiative (OPI).

The OPI was created so that we could address an array of challenges with people we work with on a daily basis. This initiative entails asking each individual or any random stranger five questions that will take about two to five minutes. This sparks so much insight and thinking that already they will become reflected positively, as it is probably something the majority of people have not thought about.

Day 208: *Support and promote local businesses that have implications for the community #PromoteLocal Business*

Day 209: *A child with autism is not ignoring you, he or she is waiting for you to enter his/her world #AutismAwareness*

So when you go up to someone, the first question would be: 1) What is your name? They will then say: "My name is John, Sally, etc." The next question is: 2) How are you? They will say: "I am well, thanks" or "I am not really having a good day." Then the next question is: 3) What challenges are you facing? Some will say they are experiencing a lot of stress at work. Some will say they are struggling to study for their exams at university or they're getting a lot of pressure from their mom and dad, or even that they are going through a divorce, that the workload is high and that their business is not doing well, etc.

The next question to ask is: 4) What is your passion in life? What do you enjoy doing in life? That is when the heartfelt answer will come out, and they will try and think about what they really do enjoy as to this day, not many people know what they enjoy or seek what their inherent strengths are. This links them to their passion in life.

Some will say, "I want to make a difference in the lives of others" or "I want to make a lot of money" or simply "love, laugh and life".

With the last question, it is tricky.

The last question is: 5) How can I (you) help? Depending on what challenges they told you about or what their passions are, a vast majority of people will say that you can help them in a financial way.

You do not want to do this as you would be treating the symptoms and not the cause. The way to treat the cause is to treat the mindset; you can do this by providing them with a sustainable idea. This is a tool that they can use to target whichever challenge they may have.

Some of them may not even have financial challenges or any other monetary constraints; they may give you a different idea on how else you can help them. So, what you want to do is think

---

Day 210: *Take someone or a group of colleagues for breakfast/coffee #BuyBreakfast4Someone*

Day 211: *"Do your little bit of good where you are; it's those little bits of good put together that overwhelm the world" – Archbishop Desmond Tutu #LittleBitOfGoodCounts*

constructively, sustainably and not in a way that is toxic by helping them for a few seconds. You want to rather leave a lasting impression on their lives so that they can make an informed decision and subsequently make a difference within their own lives. That is the best gift you can give them: engagement and also what is known as "sustainable dialogue".

If you can do that, then you can try and pass on the baton so that they can ask those same five questions to someone else. Through this, you've created a method of a sustainable pyramid humanitarian scheme. Here is the equation for the OPI using South Africa as an example.

We have approximately 60 million people. If we have to work with ordinary South Africans over a two-year period over 600 days, this will work if we had 10,000 change agents.

These agents are less than 0.002% of the population, and they could come from university or colleges around South Africa focusing on ten people per day, asking the aforementioned five questions which will not take more than 45 minutes.

As such, you will get 10,000 South African change agents asking, communicating or engaging about those five questions with ten people per day, who will hopefully become self-reformed by thinking of what they've been asked.

That would give you 100,000 people over 600 days which will bring you to the population number in South Africa of 60 million people. When you read this, you would think that it will be challenging, or that it's impossible. The word itself says: "I'm possible," according to the British actress and humanitarian Audrey Hepburn. With humanitarian activities, anything is possible if you put your mind to it. After all, our very own Mandela said: "It is not impossible until it is done".

Day 212: Spread awareness and support for cancer #SupportCancer
Day 213: International Day of Sport for Peace and Development #Peace&Development
Day 214: Encourage the importance of good health and practice #HealthyImportance

This chapter has aimed to show you the true meaning of being a humanitarian by having a heart and giving from the heart. Avoiding toxic charity and then moving towards sustainable means is key. The next chapter focuses on The Humanitarians organisation and where it started for me.

Day 215: *Keep going. Difficult roads often lead to beautiful destinations #DifficultRoads*
Day 216: *Confidence with a smile is a formidable combination #ConfidenceWithASmile*
Day 217: *Respect and appreciate all things related to Mother Earth #MotherEarth*

13

THE HUMANITARIANS

My root for community love goes back a long way. It started in high school. I will forever be indebted to my mom, dad, sister and brother for teaching me imperative values and morals, more so, for giving me a conscience for discipline and productivity. This has truly shaped me in being the driven and passionate man that I am today. Words will never be able to describe my appreciation, gratitude and love that I have for them.

Certainly, my humanitarian involvement was cultivated through my upbringing, but it was very much accentuated as I ventured into my university years. Growing up I would witness my mother invite people from the street and random strangers into our home to give them food.

This was in commemoration of various types of Islamic days. Being a Muslim, *zakat* (charity) is the third pillar of Islam and people do it very differently either through donations, giving food or a helping hand, assisting anyone in need or even just a smile. Wherever we can we try to do charity. My mom used to do this, and from a young age I grew up watching her and learnt the importance of blessings of helping people through food because with food, there is a number of blessings from a spiritual perspective.

One of the days or occasions I really remember was the "kheer and poori" day where she would invite women and children or anyone to our home to give them kheer and poori. This is a sweet

---

Day 218: Your scars tell a story, they are your natural tattoos, so choose not to remove them but to accept them and share that story to inspire others #ScarsTellStories
Day 219: The life you are living is a dream of millions – value it #ValueYourLife

dish where kheer is made from rice and milk, and poori is a dough-like substance similar to roti.

Upon completion of eating, we would wash our hands in a bucket of water so that the blessings of that food was not washed away. That was one of the imperatives of giving to the community but also to please God as well through the essence and practice of giving.

The essence of giving became a part of me from a very young age. Not only did I learn this from my mother but my father's good heart also played a role. From a young age what I saw is that my father had a heart of gold. In the sense where whenever there was an opportunity for him to help someone, he would try his best to do so or whenever there was an opportunity for him to do for his children, he would try his very best to do so.

With my brother and my sister, it was the same, where they had possibly learnt from our parents, or the family, or different friends. I grew up in a home whereby having a heart or doing something good for others was very important before doing something for yourself. This was carried on throughout my primary and high school years on a daily basis where we could help someone whenever possible. In my earlier chapters, I want to reiterate our humble beginnings, however, despite our circumstances which weren't very easy, we always strived to help people where we could whether it was for friends or family or a stranger on the street.

When I ventured into university, I thankfully got exposed to a lot more people and I think university was an environment that was really conducive for me because I was independent from a very young age. I didn't really do well in school because we had to follow the sheep (see the chapter on enemies) or we were all cultivated towards doing similar things.

For me, it was all about independence and following my own

Day 220: Spread awareness and support about Malaria #Malaria
Day 221: Choose to shine even after all the storms you've been through #ChoosetoShine
Day 222: Differentiate between rights and privileges – appreciate privileges #Privileges

route and doing something that I enjoyed. I was also a very practical person so in my second year of university I joined the Muslim Students' Association (MSA), which was one of the societies at UJ.

I served as a member during my first year but decided to get involved with the MSA on a larger scale in my second year because of the wonderful projects that they had done not only for the students but for the broader community. I learnt so much being involved in the MSA and even deliberated and communicated with other similar societies or organisations through UJ.

I decided to go through to the MSA committee and applied to become a part of the committee. Everyone voted me onto the committee, and others nominated and elected different office bearers onto the committee, which was a chairperson, vice-chairperson, treasurer and secretary. Thankfully, after a seemingly long process, I was voted as the chairperson.

Once the committee was voted in, we all had to gather into a room separate from the former committee members (which was headed by the former chairperson of the MSA during 2008, Muneer Bham).

He called for nominations of chairperson, and there were three of us: myself, Yusuf Hoosen and Akbar Mthimkhulu. We had to leave the room and there was a vote. Our committee comprised of nine of us so if the three of us went out there were only six people to vote, and three voted for myself and three voted for Yusuf.

There was a tie, and in that instance, the constitution of the MSA did not state what to do in that situation where there would be a tie when there is a vote for vice and chairperson. The current committee then decided that they would vote based on interviews that they'd had with myself and Yusuf.

It came down to me because I was a bit better in the interview.

Day 223: Practise health and safety at work #HealthandSafety
Day 224: Be a beacon of hope to the youth #BeABeaconOfHope
Day 225: Never forget your roots #NeverForgetYourRoots

They advised that I would be the new chairperson. That is how I was selected. It was a close call because Yusuf Hoosen was also remarkable in his duties and insight into the MSA.

When I started my tenure as the MSA Chairperson, I learnt so much, and we got involved with such amazing projects, one of which was the Ramadaan Humanitarian Project (RHP). RHP was a project that I had volunteered on from my matric year in 2007, and I stopped volunteering in 2011 because the month of Ramadaan had moved closer to the student holidays and so the students became less involved.

During those years, the RHP was about getting students together, 'Students Touching Humanity'. This was carried out in association with The South African National Zakaah Fund (SANZAF). We had to basically pack, distribute and collect hampers for the needy and poor. Each year a different number of hampers were packed and consolidated.

This project was started by Wits in early 2000, and it escalated as the years passed by. In my year as chairperson, there were 2 000 hampers that we had to pack amongst the Gauteng universities, including Wits, the University of Pretoria, MSA UJ and MSA Bunting (part of UJ). The four campuses had to all pack 2 000 hampers. We had to do 700 hampers, where Wits did 1 200 because they were a bigger campus.

The University of Pretoria and MSA Bunting did the remainder. This was such an amazing project where students together were touching humanity. It opened the door to what the current needs were in the community and also to understanding how such a project would work.

It was a massive project where although we were students and we would sometimes miss lectures, and we would start in the early hours of the day and finish in the late hours of the evening, it was worth it! We would always get questioned by our parents about why we were coming home late but they understood that we were doing the work of good and there was logistics involved and liaising with different types of stakeholders.

Each committee member had to do their part, liaising with trucks to deliver the goods, liaising with different companies to deliver their different types of stocks because each hamper had samp, rice, oil, different non-perishable items that would sustain a community or a house for that month of Ramadaan when they were fasting. That was the aim of this project; a hamper was going towards one household, and the aim was to feed 2 000 homes within the Johannesburg district. That is where my passion was accentuated as I got involved over a number of years in the RHP, but later on we even had different types of projects.

I moved to Cape Town in 2012. I tried to network with local organisations, but I realised that the proactivity and the drive for community work were different to Johannesburg or where I had grown up. In Gauteng, there was a lot more proactivity and drive to do good.

I struggled to network in Cape Town, and I conceptualised my own project towards exercise. Being in the field of Biokinetics, exercise was my niche area that I wanted to tap into. As most other organisations were looking at sanitation, household care, poverty, library books, education etc. I wanted to focus on a niche area involving exercise and health.

Being a biokineticist, I was an intern at the time in 2012, at the Sports Science Institute of South Africa. I wanted to start a Biokinetic project to make related services accessible to those community members who would otherwise not be able to afford it. We would

---

Day 228: *Don't estimate the work you do for the youth. Every minute counts #Don'tUnderestimateYourWork*

Day 229: *Give back in an active way #ActiveGiving*

take them through different types of screening such as exercise testing and exercise prescription. I also wanted to introduce the profession of Biokinetics into the public sector as it was only offered in the middle class / private sector. The name was formalised from the inspiration of the RHP, and called the Biokinetic Humanitarian Project (BHP).

This idea was conceptualised in 2012. Two people that I met when I got to Cape Town formed a paramount and integral part of the project at that time.

The first person that I met on 4 January 2012 was Mr Noel Adams. At the time he was the residence manager for Obz Square. I had stayed there during my first year because I was an intern biokineticist but I was also a Masters student at UCT.

Through getting to know Noel, I realised that he also had a passion for community work. Despite his culture of being a Rastafarian, he also had a passion for community. He had a sustainable way of living, and he did me a few favours when I moved to Cape Town as I did not know anyone, nor did I have a network, friends or family. In return, he humorously asked me for carrots and apples in return.

Knowing my upbringing and my surroundings growing up, if you receive a favour from someone, it is courteous to be available to help or do them a favour in return. This incredible man did not ask for money and favours. Instead, he asked for carrots and apples, and I thought he was joking, but he was actually very serious.

I went up to him the next day and actually got to sit down with him face-to-face and asked him: "Do you really want carrots and apples?"

He said: "Yes".

I then asked: "Why?"

He responded: "It is nutritious for me and that is what I eat. It is a

---

Day 230: Support local talent #SupportLocalTalent
Day 231: Challenge the youth to think critically #ThinkCritically
Day 232: You may be enemies in debate, but you are compatriots in action #BeCompatriots

sustainable way of living of eating vegetables and eating fruit." That was his 'payment' for returning a favour.

I then went and bought some apples and carrots, and he was so appreciative when I gave this to him. He told me that he does so many favours for a lot of people and not many return the favour the way he likes even though he is not a person to expect anything in return. That is when I realised that he is a true humanitarian. We kept that relationship ongoing and later on in the year on 27 April I met another fantastic human being, Taahira Moola.

The 27th of April 2012, as we know, is Freedom Day in South Africa and it was a long weekend. I was supposed to be in Durban for my cousin, Khalil Sayed's, wedding. We had a close relationship at the time and unfortunately I worked very long that night on 26 April until 9 pm and I was not able to swap my shift with another intern and tried so hard for a flight that would go and return for the wedding but I really couldn't.

I was also on shift that weekend in the gym, and it was so hard for me to swap shifts and honestly at the time, I could not afford the flights as an intern, as we only earned a salary of R3 900 per month. At that time a return ticket was in the range of R1 200 to R1 600. I did not go to Durban that weekend, and I felt so bad for Khalil and the least I could do, was pray for him.

I stayed in Cape Town doing various shifts, but it was on a Friday afternoon when I just returned from Friday prayers that I was going through my laptop. In my residence room I heard a knock on the door, and when I looked through the peephole there was a girl in a scarf standing there, which I thought was very odd. Never in history had I experienced a girl knocking on my door, besides my sister.

I opened the door. She said: "Hello".

I said: "How are you?" She asked me a question as all the students

---

Day 233: *The world would become a better place when we always consider people more important than money or materialism #PeopleAreTheTrueAssets*

Day 234: *Correct actions start with the correct thinking; correct thinking starts with the correct mindset, take action! #ThinkBeforeAct*

in the vicinity (between 8 to 12 students) were sharing the kitchen. There were three fridges in each kitchen, and we had to share a fridge between three and four people.

She had asked me which fridge I was using because she was curious about the fact that someone had thrown her meat away or had shifted her food. I basically told her that I was using a fridge which was obviously very different from the fridge she was using and I told her that I also had Halaal meat and I would never shift anyone's food or throw it away.

I greeted her, and she went away, but then she came back knocking on the door again another day, and told me that the person had done it again. Then I was really concerned, and it certainly wasn't right for them to do that. I decided to go the extra mile and tried to help her because I wouldn't want someone to do that to my food.

For the first few months, I thought that I was the only student in residence who had issues with Halaal food. From then on, we started to cook in the kitchen together and also eat together in the kitchen. From the knocking of the door on my room and eating together, we developed an amazing friendship, and it escalated and has carried on to this day. I then realised that Taahira was not just a friend, and a generous, caring person, but she was also a true humanitarian. I got to speak to her about all these projects that I had done previously, and she was always passionate about getting involved with organisations or projects that do good or focus on making a difference.

I told her about my idea. I had not told anyone about the BHP, but I explained to her how it would work. She said: "Well, why don't you start it," and she was one of those people that motivated me to 'turn this idea into practice'. We did the first BHP initiative, a pilot project at the very early stages within the student residence and we did a follow-up testing after six months. This was only conducted in the year 2013, my second year of knowing her. At that time, Noel did not know much about it but was aware of the project. In 2013, we had registered the BHP as a non-profit organisation.

When the project was registered as an NPO, we decided to carry on with a lot more projects after that. The process of registering the BHP as an NPO was such a long and frustrating process. In fact, it had taken six months to register it.

If I recall in the first batch of applications, the post office lost our application, and we had to wait very long. Only on the second attempt where we not only mailed the application but sent it via email as well, did the application eventually get through to the registrar of Pretoria to register it as an NPO.

We received our registration certificate a few weeks after that, finally! We carried on the BHP and other projects, and by this time Noel had joined us, and we also got to see the work that he did on an informal basis and a non-structured capacity in the community. He has taught us so much regarding sustainability, innovation, green campaigns, etc. We were so inspired by all the projects he had done.

He taught us the idea of a sustainable clay oven and a heater amongst other things. He shared with us his work done with the prostitutes on the streets, prisoners from Pollsmoor Prison and the fact that he had gone to shopping malls and when the people went to pay for their parking tickets, he would offer to pay by giving them R5 coins.

Mind you, this man was not well-off; he was just like me at the time, a working-class man but with a heart to help people. He used to basically save some money every month so that he could bank a lot of R5 coins and help people pay for their parking or even buy a

---

Day 237: *To the world you are a mother, but to your family you are the world #AppreciateYourMother*

Day 238: *Do more chores and duties around the house to lessen the load on your dad #AppreciateYourFather*

lot of naartjies or oranges and pass them out.

That was ironic because in the community when you call someone a "naartjie", you are implying that they are a prostitute. It was something that I learnt very quickly, among the other jokes and stereotypical language used in the rural areas. They referred to prostitutes as naartjies because they are "easy to squeeze". We slowly demotivated the communities from using this derogatory term because it came across as insulting and inappropriate for the masses. As you can imagine, it caused quite a stir in schools, churches, the communities and its surrounding areas (it still does).

It was these acts of kindness taught by Noel that were so simple but made such a difference to people, that cause me to say: "Okay, we have to get Noel involved." I witnessed his small acts of kindness as massive messages to involve him, without the need of having to see his Curriculum Vitae or interview him.

I then approached him with the idea that we already had a registered organisation, the BHP, but after working with him and deliberating, we had realised that there are other settings in need where we could make a difference and not just within the Exercise Sciences. We sat down, and we brainstormed and thought of ideas, and after a long few days, whether I was in the shower or the car (usually the great ideas come to me when I shower), I thought about branding and naming our new NPO: The Humanitarians.

It was a very simple name; I wanted to keep it that way because our long-term vision was to inspire and teach people how to become humanitarians or inspire them to have a Humanitarian Heart.

We had to then file an amendment to the NPO and the Constitution that already existed and that again, took very long to process. Our amendment of the name to The Humanitarians was a tedious process, but it felt like a huge load off our shoulders once

---

Day 239: The role of families goes beyond just promoting education and overall well-being of their members #Families

Day 240: A successful 'DRROP' involves diligence, respect, responsibility, organisation and planning #DRROP

approved.

This was when I, and the team knew that this was our calling and something we had all been waiting for and working towards. Through The Humanitarians we could do small projects and random acts of kindness because The Humanitarians had started off as a volunteer-based organisation (and it still is).

We have not received main-stream funding nor have we received substantial subsidies from organisations or corporate social investments. A lot of our projects were done on a volunteer basis or even at times through our own pockets, where we could, to sustain the organisation and running expenses.

With The Humanitarians and working together with these individuals, we will always be known as the awesome threesome, myself, Noel and Taahira. Together we formed a formidable tripod, and we still do. There were a number of people who were interested in volunteering with us and although it was admirable to have received this interest, their time with us was quite short, and they felt stagnant. It went from a period of two days to two months.

That was it, and it was not longer than that. They realised that for the work that we did you really needed to have the heart, spirit and mind. It meant going into the community, and not many people are able to handle the emotional perspective of what was witnessed nor endure some of the physical requirements. So we have had a number of volunteers who have come and gone.

We realised that a lot of these volunteers wanted to also receive a salary from our organisation even though we were upfront and thorough from the beginning that this was a volunteer-based organisation. Even we did not receive a cent from being involved in our own organisation over the last four years.

The three of us have always remained the integral pillars of The

---

Day 241: *Educate people on the prevention of hypertension and how to take blood pressure #Hypertension*

Day 242: *Always put your trust in God. God always holds your hands but at times, we don't hold back #TrustInGod*

Humanitarians, bouncing ideas off one another, doing work for one another, forming policies, constitutions in terms of need and this is what has strengthened our relationship till today. The projects that we have done eventually diversified into five main sectors: Sport, Health, Education, Sustainability and Innovation.

The slogan for our organisation is "Creating a sustainable and innovative society." The reason for these words comes from the experiences I had when working on the MSA and SANZAF. We got to learn about a concept called 'toxic charity.' This is a concept that describes that if I give you bread today and if I don't see you tomorrow, where will you get that bread from tomorrow?

Or if I do something with you tomorrow, what will you do after that? A lot of projects in communities need to be sustainable because people need to sustain their health, living, livelihood, income, access to water, food, employment, education etc. and everything needs to be sustainable. There are many projects out there, and though admirable, they are not focusing on the sustenance and sustainability of the projects but are rather focused on a one-day programme or a quick fix.

That is known as toxic charity. The second reason why we used the word innovation is that we realised that we needed to base the organisation within innovation. With the rapid evolvement of technology and modernisation, we realised that innovation had evolved tremendously over time. Innovation is what is required to lay the foundation for fantastic work to be achieved in the future. By utilising improved technology, we are able to make life easier and sustainable. That is the reason for the logo which focuses on five spheres on each finger.

We are one of the very few organisations, with the uniqueness of measuring and tracking the impact and progress of our projects

---

Day 243: *Support, follow and like the inspiring individuals #SupportOtherInspirers*

Day 244: *Being a male is a matter of birth. Being a man is a matter of age. But being a gentleman is a matter of choice – Vin Diesel. Stop abusing women and children #BeAGentleman*

through research. Taahira and I are academics at university, which complements our portfolio in that we have a background not only in reporting but also in research methodology. It is very important that our projects are measured in this way so that we can inform corporates, industry and government about our findings and the impact and the implications to society, the gaps and where improvements are needed and what the weaknesses are.

A number of projects have been carried out under the umbrella of The Humanitarians. These have included frail care, exercise, Biokinetics, health, the One-Person-Initiative, random acts of kindness, the destitute, the sustainable book project, embracing dignity and other projects focusing on sustainability.

The fundamental question is: Where are The Humanitarians today? We always struggled to get funding and exposure for many years either because we didn't have a public benefit organisation (PBO) certificate or the fact that we probably did not fit the dimensions and criteria of most corporate or funding companies.

The good news is, as of September 2017 and after much patience, The Humanitarians is now a public benefit organisation. This means that The Humanitarians can now have more opportunities of attracting funding sources to do more good work on a higher level.

Irrespective of the reasons for not getting funding or exposure in previous years, we have continued to pave the way forward and make a difference through our projects. A few of my friends suggested that I should enter the Mr South Africa competition. I looked at them with a very puzzled face saying, "How could you suggest that to me, have you seen the way that I look? I am not a model and do not fit the criteria of a Mr South Africa."

I responded in this way because growing up I remember watching Miss South Africa and Miss Universe and I knew that it was all about height, beauty, the way you look and how you modelled. Honestly, for me, I had none of that. Some people may say that I was good looking, but I don't think that I was on that level of beauty. I thought long and hard about it after liaising with a number of my friends and family.

My mum had outright said 'no' because it was not within the confinements of Islam and Shariah. My sister said 'no' at the time because she did not look beyond the pageant.

My brother had researched the brand quite thoroughly and advised that 'it's all about what you make of it', explaining to me and using Hashim Amla as a formidable example. He is a great cricket player but refused the Castle Lager sign, and he continues the etiquette and principles of Islam throughout his cricket career. My brother said that with this platform I could do something similar where you conform to your morals and your values and that you can break the stereotype. After thinking about it for some time, I said I would enter and see how far I would get.

I entered the Mr South Africa platform to evoke a sustainable and innovative change in the lives of others but also to serve as a springboard to The Humanitarians NPO. This is why I entered, to use the platform to elevate brand awareness of the organisation and give it a lot more credibility so that we could attract a lot more funding and exposure through broader channels. It was not just for personal limelight to leverage my career, but the primary reason for entering was for The Humanitarians.

Day 247: Every mountain top is within reach if you just keep climbing #KeepClimbing
Day 248: You can either bring people down or lift them up, choose the latter #LiftUp
Day 249: A weak man does not cry, a strong man does #CryingIsNotWeakness

14

MR SOUTH AFRICA

Where it all started

The Mr South Africa journey started for me in March 2015. I was inspired by a few people to enter. My first impression of the Mr South Africa competition was that it was about models and/or about having an appealing physique. After doing some research I took note of the past winners, one of whom was Michael Mol.

He was one of the guys who stood out for me because he came from a similar background and had a similar career path that I did in terms of education, making a difference in the community, as well as being an aspirational presenter.

I had followed the Mr South Africa brand for a few weeks and I gave it quite a bit of thought before entering. I said: "Let me take the plunge and see if I can use this platform to evoke a sustainable difference in society." Towards the end of March 2015, I entered Mr South Africa and looked forward to taking part in the competition during the year. We were required to carry out a few challenges.

Challenge one was focused on advertising and challenge two was focused towards signing up of memberships. The aim of the Mr South Africa challenges was to take you out of your comfort zone,

---

Day 250: Help the less fortunate during Yom Kippur #YomKippur
Day 251: Sustain a community for the month of Ramadaan #Ramadaan

and make you grow and learn new skills along the way through varied avenues. Unfortunately, the competition came to a pause and I thought then that it was the end of the road in terms of Mr South Africa for me. I was also quite busy with my academics, other humanitarian work, as well as with my Ph.D. To be honest, Mr South Africa was not the main priority in my life at the time.

Later in May 2016, I was in London for a conference and I was also doing some research testing for my Ph.D. when all of a sudden while I was catching a train from Cricklewood to The Oval cricket stadium, I was added to a WhatsApp group called Mr South Africa 2016 and I was amazed.

Wow, is this still happening? I wondered.

I thought it was done and dusted but it seemed that some of the guys had actually followed through from the 2015 to the 2016 group. I remembered the guys very fondly; most of those who had stayed on from 2015, had become close friends of mine. For one of the challenges in 2015 I did not raise enough money although I tried my best and raised as much as I could. Subsequently, I got an email from the Mr South Africa CEO, saying: "Unfortunately you have not made the Top 25. You have been eliminated from the competition. We hope that this doesn't demotivate you from entering in the future."

I wrote an elimination appeal letter to state all the work I had done and all the effort I had put into the competition. I also appealed to Mr South Africa organisers to 're-consider my elimination' as I felt that I could really make a difference in South Africa.

The CEO accepted the appeal letter and re-instated me into the competition. Thereafter, I did not hear anything. I believe some of the guys who didn't make it to the Top 25 had also sent appeal letters and that five of us out of the 30 odd were carried on to 2016.

Day 252: Understand what a hungry person goes through on a daily basis and fast for a day #Fasting
Day 253: Give blankets to those in need or who are deprived of warmth #Blankets

Of those guys who made the Top 25, I'm not sure if they had exited the competition or if they no longer wanted to participate because there was a break in 2015 and we only carried on in 2016.

Give It Another Shot

When it started again in May 2016, I wondered once more if I should stay in the competition. I was very busy with work, my Ph.D. and with The Humanitarians. I decided to give it a month or two and then assess how it was going and how much I could learn from this competition.

The turning point for me was when Zelda Kraftt (who today is a good friend of mine), the General Manager of Mr South Africa at the time, asked the Cape Town contestants if they would like to be present on June 16th 2016 for Youth Day to give an inspirational talk to the youth in one of the communities, Bishops Lavis, in Cape Town. I felt strongly about continuing at this stage as this forms part of my humanitarian conscience. Inspiring the youth is what I love doing! When I did, I met two other contestants who have become close brothers until today, Heinrich Gabler (who has entered Mr South Africa again – I hope he does well!) and Brendt Wayne DeWet (fellow Top 5 Mr South Africa 2016 finalist).

I thought, *these guys are actually cool so I'm going to stick around in this competition as long as I can*. Because few of us had already been a part of the 2015 competition, we were exempt from the first two challenges which automatically gave us the opportunity to go through to the next round of Top 25. I was also concerned about being exposed to guys who might be slightly narcissist or arrogant. Brendt and Heinrich were definitely not. The 'real competition' started from challenge three when we were all expected to carry out the same challenge irrespective of whether we entered in 2015 or 2016. As there were no exceptions, we all felt that we were treated equally.

Challenge three was about doing a random act of kindness (RAK) and we had to do a RAK to a specific person or an organisation for 30 days. We were assessed around what we had done. At the end of challenge three we had to turn in a strategic plan of what we had done and what our goals were.

We had to consider what we would do with the title of Mr South Africa, if we were to win the competition. Our responses were then scored. The Top 25 were scored and they were going to eliminate two guys from the competition. I enjoyed that challenge so much as I had been doing humanitarian work and acts of kindness since 2013. I was ranked number one for the Top 23 challenge.

I thank Yakeen Sadiq for assisting me with mentorship during that time period. He has fundamental unique skills of coaching and marketing that would easily place him in the top 20% of businessmen that I have come across. Unfortunately, two guys from the Top 25 had not made it. I think that challenge three was a massive turning point in the competition for me.

It reassured me to stick around a lot longer and I thought that if I did a lot more work I could probably make the finals. The goal for me was to make the finals because I knew that if I made the finals for the Mr South Africa competition I would have created a lot more contacts and leverage through the platform, which in turn would help me make more of a difference to The Humanitarians NPO and its brand.

I decided to carry on and it was a massive confidence boost for me, making the Top 23 and being ranked number one. It also

---

Day 257: Surround yourself with like-minded individuals #LikeMindedIndividuals
Day 258: Teach a child or person how to read #Reading
Day 259: Encourage and involve kids in fun activities #FunforKids

reassured a lot of people as well who were following my journey that 'it wasn't just about the six pack abs or muscle'. It was about brawn and heart rather than beauty.

The next challenge really took me out of my comfort zone.

Challenge four was a fundraiser to raise a minimum of R10,000 for a charity. I thought of many ideas of how we could put together a fun fundraiser. Through our projects focusing on sustainability I came up with the idea of Sustainable Laughter. We decided on this project because we know that a lot of people especially in Cape Town love to laugh. As South Africans we have two richness's, namely embracing our cultural diversity of four different races and the second, which you cannot match anywhere in the world, is our sense of humour. We really love to laugh, so this was to be a fun fundraiser.

However, the reason why this challenge was so tough for me is because we had already secured a sponsor for the challenge. From the two sponsors we had secured R20,000 collectively. Closer to the time, a week before the actual fundraiser at the Cape Town Comedy Club, these companies pulled out because we did not have a Section 18A certificate. The Humanitarians at that time was not registered as a Public Benefit Organisation (PBO) and we couldn't issue Section 18A certificates. We had lost that R20,000 and I was in a huge panic. In a week, how was I going to raise R10,000 profit? The minimum allocation of tickets that we had to sell for the comedy club was 150 and to be honest we had only sold 35. At the very last minute, I was contacting people from all sorts of companies and organisations to try to get donations and fortunately a lot of people were generous and provided their donations and we were allowed to then give out complimentary tickets to get our minimum allocated number of 150 seated people.

Day 260: Care for the earth and become green agents for change #Environment
Day 261: Celebrate the success of others #CelebrateTheSuccessofOthers

And so we held the Sustainable Laughter event at the Cape Town Comedy Club and we not only raised the desired amount of money but also created a lot of brand awareness and exposure for the Mr South Africa brand but especially also for The Humanitarians. Through the tough two months on that project, we had networked and made contacts with 70 companies in Cape Town.

We met so many people and gained much credibility towards the organisation. This was actually the first fundraising project that we had done through the Mr South Africa platform and when I made it through to the Top 14 or after the challenge was done, I knew the Mr South Africa brand had assisted us. It was not only through this challenge; it was also through the RAK from challenge three.

When I made it as a finalist I knew my goal with Mr South Africa was achieved. I reached my goal of getting exposure, funding opportunities or leverage for The Humanitarians. If I were to get voted out during the Top 14, I would leave the competition with pride, humility and honour.

This is what the Mr South Africa platform did for us; it pushed us out of our comfort zone to take us through to the next level. If we did not have anyone challenging us then we wouldn't even have been sure if we had in fact gone through another challenge.

This is what my life has stood for; it was not about limits but plateaus. It was always about taking it to the next level and this fundraiser had presented us with red tape and obstacles. Fortunately, from that list of 70 contacts we had received a number of donations and that's where we were able to volunteer 100 tickets to friends, non-profit organisations and the general public to reach our minimum allocation.

The Cape Town Comedy Club fee with an audio-visual fee and Comedians fee was R12,500. We had raised R20,000 on the night

---

***Day 262**: Send flowers to an administrative colleague to show your appreciation for all that they do #Flowers*
***Day 263**: Help clean swimming pools or the ocean #Ocean*

and R11,000 went to Mr South Africa and R1,500 went to The Humanitarians. Once again, we did not receive a cent from this since it was a volunteer-based project. It was a lesson that out of the 70 contacts you gain on a daily basis, only two or three will come through and that is what we had.

Through this process the person that really contributed a lot of the time, energy and effort into this project was Taahira Moola. You know that this is where you don't really see a lot of people with the heart of a humanitarian. She is part of a vast minority. She really puts so much of her time and effort into this project but also for The Humanitarians. She was the rock of that project and remains today the rock of The Humanitarians organisation. The amount of administration work she does, emails and deliberations she undertakes with stakeholders, behind the scenes and the type of person she is, the way she maintains it behind the scenes is exemplary from what I have seen in any other person. A lot of credit once again must be given to her.

With the Humanitarians right now, without the Mr South Africa platform and valuable contacts, this all could not have been achieved. Before entering the Mr South Africa competition we would get a lot of resistance from people we contacted for funding or partnerships.

Having a title like Mr South Africa, people are more responsive and positive towards ideas and want to assist where they can **but only** because of the title. It is very unfortunate that in society only when you get to a certain status or title, that is where people leverage because at the end of the day, businesses want to benefit from it. That is the world we live in and that is the current status of The Humanitarians, trying to use a title as best we can to benefit The Humanitarians as much as possible, thus benefiting our society

---

Day 264: Most of life is impromptu, be ready for the unexpected #Impromptu
Day 265: Understanding is deeper than knowledge. There are many people who know you, but there are very few who understand you #UnderstandMore

and making a difference.

Through these testing times, God was great, the evening was a huge success and 162 people were in attendance. It was a fabulous night with Schalk Bezuidenhout as the lead act and Mel Jones as the Master of Ceremonies.

Some of the monies raised from challenge four allowed us to do a project in Bonteheuwel on exercise and health.

After submitting the report for challenge four, I was then ranked number five and I made the Top 14. I thought to myself: "Wow, I made the finals of the Mr South Africa competition after 80 contestants had entered initially from March 2015 until 2016." That is when I went through to the finals but my goal was never to win, I never had that expectation or even to be in the Top 5 for that matter.

To be honest, I actually was apprehensive in the initial stages because I didn't have the height, muscles or the six-pack to win. I knew that the competition was looking for that x-factor and my x-factor was probably the questions asked on the evening. During the rehearsals of the finals night I also noticed that a lot of the guys at the rehearsal were not smiling and were rather showing their muscles and physique. My x-factor was going to be my natural smile (I had nothing to really show).

To take it one step back, I had won Mr Carnival in Grade 4 when I was nine years old. I entered the Mr Carnival competition (purely a fun event at a school festival) and I had the exact same feeling as I did for the Mr South Africa finals, "let me just enter this for fun and see how far I can get."

At the Mr Carnival competition even at nine years old, guys were a bit egocentric and narcissistic. They did activities on stage that a lot of other guys loved but at that young age and having played

Day 266: Raise funds for the destitute during winter #HelpTheDestitute
Day 267: Spread awareness against child labour #SayNoToChildLabour
Day 268: Eliminate violence against women #ViolenceAgainstWomen

sport from a very young age, I always knew that I had to do something different. I had to show that x-factor or uniqueness but more so I had to be authentic and be myself.

My sister, Khatija, had given the simplest yet the greatest advice that she could to a nine-year-old. She had said, "Habib, smile, just keep smiling, you are the only one who is smiling on stage, keep smiling." And you know what? I was crowned as Mr Carnival at the E.P. Baumann Primary School in Johannesburg. In my family, it wasn't a major thing, it was a light giggle and 'well done'.

I even remember my brother, who was in first year Medical School at the time, saying: "Tops, well done! How you did that?"

I took on that same advice that I had remembered from my sister, 19 years ago, 'Habib, smile...' That was probably one of the x-factors that I had on that night, that I had smiled. I was a bit confident and my answer to the first question that was asked (simple question: Why enter Mr. South Africa?) had really taken the audience by surprise. Those were the x-factors, I believe, which I think made me win.

Preparation for Mr South Africa 2016 Finals

When acquiring a health and fitness goal, the concept of individuality is key. At some point, people who have trained for a long time get accustomed to their bodies and know how their bodies would respond to various exercises, eating habits, sleep and recovery.

In essence, certain exercises or eating regimes that one does cannot be based on a mesocycle (short-term based). It has to be consistent and form part of one's lifestyle. However, when athletes and individuals are preparing for sports or events, the last four weeks of preparations are crucial in leveraging their performance. I

Day 269: Donate blood and help save a life #DonateBlood
Day 270: Build strong support against the abuse of the elderly #ElderAbuseAwareness
Day 271: Provide assistance to someone by helping them reach their goals #Goals

call it: from the fourth to fifth gear of training.

Among other qualities, Mr South Africa is striving to find the perfect aspirational man; balanced in health with a fit physique. One can define health in numerous ways. For example, if you have rock hard abs and are well defined, are you healthy? No, this implies a fit and adequate physique. Health can incorporate various clinical and health measures such as normal: blood pressure ranges, heart rate, glucose, cholesterol and body fat percentage. If one has an FBC (full blood count) done at the hospital, one would be able to gauge one's health values ranging from cholesterol and triglycerides, to kidney function, liver function, white and red blood cell counts and more. I ultimately believe, that if these are within normal ranges, then one can define oneself as healthy.

Moving on to my personal four-week preparation for the Mr South Africa finals, which took place on the 24th November at the Rand Airport in Johannesburg; it involved smart training, a low carbohydrate eating plan, adequate sleep and pre- and post-measurements.

Smart Training
- **Frequency:** 5 days / week (gym) and 1 day active rest (walking/ hike) and 1 day complete rest
- **Intensity:** Moderate to high
- **Type:** Endurance-based with an emphasis on strength
- **Duration:** between 60 and 90 minutes all-inclusive

Cardio
20 minutes on either cycle or treadmill, alternating between 5 days
Treadmill: Speed – between 10 and 13; Incline – 1; Programme – normal
Upright cycle ergometer: Speed – above 100 rpm; Level – 2/3

Day 272: Life is a circle of happiness, sadness, hard times and good times #LifeCircle
Day 273: Every sport has a history, understand and appreciate it #HistoryOfSport

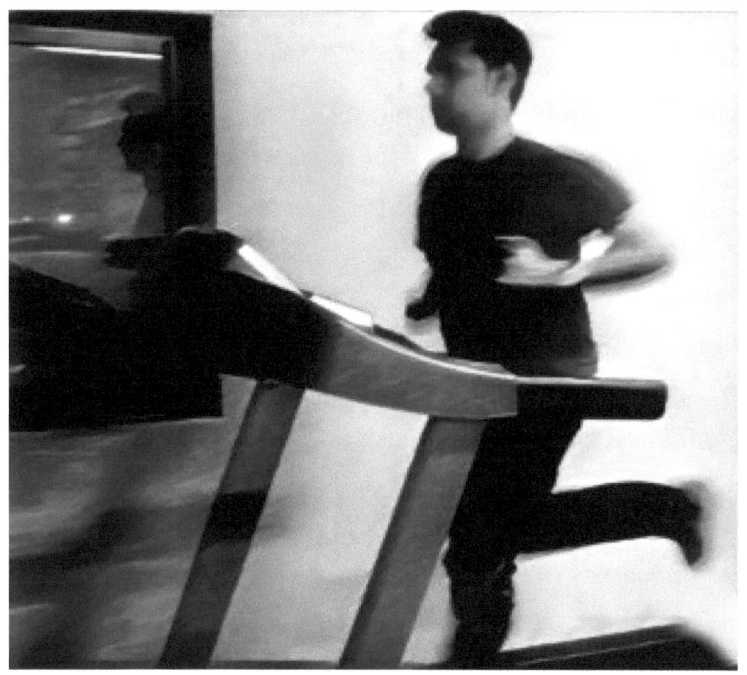

Weight Training
- Bicep curls 2 x 10 reps
- Tricep overhead extensions 2 x 10 reps
- One-arm bent over-row 2 x 12 reps
- Chest press 2 x 10 reps
- Shoulder press 2 x 10 reps
- Push up with weight and burpee 2 x 20
- Front squat with weight 2 x 10

Plyometrics
- Split squats 2 sets x 10
- Lunges with weight 2 sets x 15
- Three-medicine ball push-ups 2 x 8
- Box jumps 2 x 12

Abdominals
- Box jumps 2 x 12
- Mountain climbers 2 x 1 minute
- Russian twists 2 x 30
- Ab curls with weights 2 x 30
- Planks 3 x 1-minute

Swimming
I swam 12 laps (50 metres length) after training. These included freestyle, backstroke, breast-stroke and butterfly (3 each).

Note: I did the above on all five days. For me, consistency where my body becomes accustomed to this on a routine basis was key.

Low Carbohydrate Eating Plan
There is a lot of debate in the nutritional field, where if one needs to build muscle, then one needs to have a required amount of carbohydrates for energy. I am not a dietician but I am a Sports Scientist. Research has recently emerged to show the evidence behind the association of low carbohydrates on sport performance / training.

The basics of nutrition have taught us that one gram of carbohydrate provides 4k/cal, while one gram of protein provides 4k/cal and one gram of fat provides 9k/cal. One can still rely on healthy fats as a reserve source of energy fuel. Throughout the week, I choose from my three meal plans. Remember, this eating plan works for me and it may not work for you nor am I trying to advise or impose anyone to follow it. If further advice or guidelines are needed, please consult with a dietician.

Day 276: Spread awareness and provide education on psoriasis #Psoriasis
Day 277: Practise some meditation and spread the beneficial messages of yoga #Yoga

Option 1:
Breakfast: 2 boiled eggs and 1 cup of coffee with full-fat cream
Snacks: biltong throughout the day
Lunch: Tuna with cottage cheese or Tuna with avocado and coriander
Supper: ½ chicken with vegetables (broccoli, cauliflower and pumpkin) and mushroom sauce

Option 2:
Breakfast: same as Option 1
Snacks: Almonds
Lunch: Tuna with cottage cheese or Tuna with avocado and coriander
Supper: 250g steak with sweet potato and pumpkin

Option 3:
Breakfast: same as option 1 and 2
Snacks: Mixed berries and Yoghurt
Lunch: Tuna with cottage cheese or Tuna with avocado and coriander
Supper: Fish with spinach and cream cheese

Note: breakfasts and lunches stay the same (consistency) but suppers and snacks vary (so that it's not monotonous). Two litres of water is consumed throughout the day.

Sleep

On average, 7 hours per night. This can range between 6 and 8 hours depending on the day in the week.

Mind-set

To prepare mentally, I pray, watch comedy 30 minutes a day, read at least 2 hours a day (journal articles, blogs, a book, etc.) and

---

Day 278: Help the youth come out of their shell and express their inherent strengths #InherentStrengths
Day 279: *Spread awareness and provide support to those suffering from epilepsy #Epilepsy*

drive for at least 30 minutes during the day to improve my attention focus.

Pre- and post-measurements
Body fat percentage
Weight / BMI
Glucose
Blood pressure
Heart rate
Arm girth
Waist circumference
Hip circumference
Chest circumference
Calf circumference
Thigh circumference
Push ups per minute
Sit ups per minute

The Finals

Something to take note of was that I nearly withdrew from the competition. Two nights before the final on the 24 November 2016 (we had flown to Johannesburg on 22 November, on my birthday), we had been briefed on what to expect with the competition and the five scenes we were going to do and what clothing we were going to wear. One of the things that I was always dreading throughout the competition was the fact that I would have to take my clothes off and do the underwear scene.

I was really dreading this because that is not who I am and not why I entered the competition and I had never entered a pageant before in my life. This was my first pageant or modelling exposure. I went straight into the deep end with Mr South Africa. In 1998, Mr Carnival was a fun competition, not a pageant. I had also never modelled before in my life. I knew nothing of how or what to do and the underwear scene was brought up when we had spoken two days before the final.

I had put up my hand and told the organisers: "I am very uncomfortable modelling in underwear and it's not who I am and I don't want to be someone that I am not. With the greatest respect and humility, I would like to withdraw from the competition." Quite a few of the other guys were very surprised and another good friend of mine, Louis Pieterse, also shared the same sentiment as I did.

The underwear sponsor was present and was quite surprised at what I had said.

The organisers spoke and came back with a surprising response. They probably did not want to lose any of their contestants on the final night as they had already arranged outfits for the Top 14. So they came back and said: "We are going to include trunks and a vest into the underwear scene." It was a huge relief when they said that as I didn't have to quit. Internally, I was so thankful.

On the final night we had to choose between a speedo or trunks and I obviously took the trunks as it was a bit longer and wasn't showing too much coupled with wearing the vest. That increased my confidence and I felt a lot more comfortable. I had nearly withdrawn from the competition because I had always maintained my moral code and had always maintained my principles throughout the competition.

Another aspect that is important to mention is that I had no idea how to model. The night before the finals, I had watched some

Day 282: *The shadow is the greatest teacher for how to come to the light – Ram Dass #shadow*
Day 283: *Life can only be understood backwards; but it must be lived forwards #Life&Living*

YouTube videos or Fashion TV of how men were strutting on the catwalk or how they were walking down the ramp. I had no idea how to do it; I knew how to walk but I did not know how to model or walk down a ramp.

I had received a few guidelines from people saying, "open up your shoulders, show your chest but not in an arrogant manner, stand upright, maintain eye contact, etc." For me, when I went on the stage those three things were the main important things: walk with confidence, maintain eye contact with the judges and the audience, and smile all the time.

I knew that those would be the x-factors and we were told that the judges were looking for an x-factor, something different. If I could be myself and do those three things since I could not show any muscles, as it was not me and not the type of person I was, then when on stage the judges would be able to see if I was being true to myself (authenticity) and I had to do just that, be true to who I am and be the best version of myself.

Later that evening, I won the title of Mr Heart South Africa, for all the charity projects and initiatives done as a contestant. That for me, was a humble recognition. But that was not all. The Top 5 was also announced. As mentioned earlier, my goal was to make the finals and I had already achieved what I set out to do.

When they called my name in the Top 5, I was stunned. The five of us were then asked additional questions. I was asked by one of the judges: "Name one challenge you faced in your life and how you overcame it". I thought for three seconds and then answered: *"Thank you very much for the question and it is an honour for me to be in the top 5. My greatest accomplishment in my life, I believe, is my relationships with people. The main challenge I faced in my life is establishing and then maintaining relationships with people. What I*

Day 284: Give thank you cards to health professionals, as they save lives every day #HealthProfessionals

Day 285: Don't underestimate the value and strength of nurses, they are the beating heart of hospitals #Nurses

had particularly found challenging is that quite positively, people are different and unique in their own way. Specifically in South Africa, our richness is our cultural diversity. Initially I had found that to be challenging when approaching or communicating with people. However, I learnt to overcome this challenge by being kind, diplomatic and using tact when possible. I had later learnt that relationships with people are not a challenge, but instead your greatest asset."

After I had answered the question, I was confident that this would allow me to make the Top 3. The Top 3 was then announced and I had a mild feeling of being the 2nd or 1st runner up. However, JP Roberts was announced as the 2nd runner up and then Diaan Neethling was announced as the 1st runner up. It was then myself, Brendt Wayne de Wet and Louis Pieterse who were left.

I was standing in the middle and on both my sides, Brendt and Louis were there. We huddled up. Both of them whispered in my ear, "This is yours Habib."

And I said, "No guys, it can be any of us". Gerry Elsdon was the MC that night and till today I can hear her voice in my head when she made the following announcement: *"And your Mr South Africa for 2017 is... Habib Noorbhai!"*

I immediately lifted my hands to my face with disbelief. I remember feeling dreamy or as if it were an illusion. Was this really happening? I then saw former Mr South Africa, Armand du Plessis walking towards me with the sash. He congratulated me and I thanked him for being a wonderful inspiration and setting a good example to all of us. He put the sash around me, I shook his hand and I walked down the ramp to thank and show my appreciation to the crowd.

I had never worn a sash before in my life. When I walked back to congratulate and greet my fellow top 5 finalists, half of my sash fell

---

Day 286: *Life is brighter when the mind is open #HaveAnOpenMind*
Day 287: *Being the same person privately, publicly and personally = authenticity #Authenticity*

off my left shoulder. I had no idea how to control the sash.

The rest of the evening was enjoyable from having my picture taken to being interviewed by the press and various television channels such as *Top Billing*, to being hugged and congratulated.

My brother and dad were at the finals and we later went up to the room to absorb the moment, laugh about it and have a brief chat. My brother was really happy and proud. My dad said: "Habib, well done. What does this mean now?"

I chuckled and said, "Dad, I now have a better platform to do more good work for others."

He said: "Okay, that's good. What did you win?"

That's the catch... Believe it or not, I won the prestigious title of Mr South Africa (very humbled and grateful), a leather bag, a gym membership and some vests and shorts. I will always be grateful for winning the prestigious title. Unfortunately, the public had the perception that I would have won money, a car, etc.

However, Mr South Africa and Miss South Africa are different brands. The difference is that Miss South Arica is backed by corporate sponsors whereas Mr South Africa is not. According to some articles that I have read, Miss South Africa won cash, a car and other prizes. Mr South Africa was opposite. It is two different brands. Many are baffled when I tell them that I haven't won anything but it's the truth. But I am certain that I will be rewarded ten-fold in some other way, but even then, I will have no expectations.

My goal with Mr South Africa wasn't to win anything in monetary value or materialistically. My goal in life is to make a difference and this is the purpose of my life that I fortunately identified a long time ago.

After having the conversation and some advice from my brother and dad, I informed them that there was an after party and it wouldn't be right if I did not attend.

Day 288: Balance is not something you find, it's something you create #Balance

Day 289: Align yourself with people who have a similar drive, synergy and proactivity #Alignment

The first hour as Mr South Africa

I had no idea where the after party was. I knew it wasn't very far from the event but had no idea where it was. My dad said he was tired (it was midnight) so just my brother and myself decided that we would go. After asking the security guards at the Dakota Lodge at the Rand Airport, they informed us that it was a bit of a walk. We should drive.

They then pointed towards the second robot down the road and said, "You must turn right there and go straight." – the greatest words of direction in South Africa. I could see the robot from where we were standing and I told Aslam, "Let's walk quickly, I am sure it is not that far."

The security guard then said, "It's also not safe this time of the night so you should rather take a car."

My brother and I walked. We walked quickly and eventually turned right at the second robot. As we were walking up the road, we saw nothing; we didn't even hear any party sounds or any music. There was a police car slowly approaching us. I suggested we ask them if they knew anything or where this place could be.

Before I could even stop them to ask, they had already stopped to interrogate us. They thought we were probably up to no good or carrying some intoxicants of some sort. At the time, my Mr South Africa sash was in my jacket pocket. They asked: "Where are you guys going?"

Aslam said, "We're going to the Mr South Africa after party".

The policeman said: "Mr what?" My brother spoke again and explained.

The policeman asked: "Mr South Africa? Where is he?"

I looked at Aslam smiling.

Day 290: Likes, comments and shares should never be your intention; your goal should be to inspire. Even if it's one person per day, you've done the ordinary. If it's more, it's a blessing from God which makes it extraordinary #Inspire

Day 291: Wish local designers all the best and praise models #LocalDesigners

Aslam grinned at me, and said: "Here he is."

Policeman: "This one? Mr South Africa? Can't be…"

They then searched us. My brother is a general surgeon, and he had his medical identification cards in his wallet. They asked whether my brother was a doctor or not and if he was using these fake cards to get drugs at this time of the night. I was laughing so hard inside but I was also in disbelief.

They couldn't come to terms with the fact that my brother was a surgeon because he looked young for his age. They then searched me and they found the sash in my pocket. I was thinking, *please don't take it, I just got it!* They asked, "Awww, is this where you are keeping your guys drugs, ehh?" The policeman opened it and saw while spelling it out: "M i s t e r S o u t h A f r i c a! You??"

I said, "Yes boetie."

Policeman: "Yoh – I am sorry neh! Where do you need to go?"

After trying to explain about the after party and where we needed to be, we finally found it. We even got the policeman some coffee and water as a thank you for taking us, otherwise we probably would have never found it.

The security guard at Dakota Lodge gave us the wrong directions. I so wish I had known where the after party was BEFORE the event had commenced. In that frame of mind, I was in preparation mode for the final and we were busy with rehearsals.

My brother and I got out, and we laughed so hard. My brother said, "Go and greet everyone, I'll go get the cops their coffee and drinks and I will come in after." I then went inside and greeted everyone and had a wonderful welcome. A night that I will never forget!

My first hour as Mr South Africa was indeed an interesting one.

Day 292: *Work for a cause, not for applause. Live life to express, not to impress #CauseAndExpress*

Day 293: *Happiness lies in Wilderness, not in civilization #Wilderness*

My reign as Mr South Africa 2017

I was obviously overwhelmed at all of the messages received over the night. I barely slept a wink that night I won. I probably got two or three hours of sleep but yet I was still a bit energised. The adrenalin had carried through. In one night, I received over 500 Facebook friend requests, more than 150 WhatsApp messages, 430 tagged posts on Facebook, 75 tagged tweets, countless emails and a number of missed calls.

It took me a few days to respond to all. But I learnt very quickly how to overcome this overwhelming moment and being in the spotlight after my first post as Mr South Africa, had made some newspapers and online news.

I had said:

"Good morning South Africa and to friends around the world :)

I barely slept a wink last night. Words can't describe the emotions that are going through me at the moment. What I can say is that I'm truly humbled, appreciative and grateful to have achieved this prestigious title; in which any of the other amazing 13 men of honour could have also achieved. It was such an honour to have shared the stage, journey and platform with all of them. We know that our work does not stop and as Armand said last night, let's keep that flame burning.

There are so many people to thank along this journey leading up to the finals; friends, family, colleagues, the Mr South Africa team, my partners and sponsors, and to everyone for your words of congratulations! I highly appreciate it ☺

To Armand du Plessis, thanks for being an inspiration to us all and for a splendid reign! You really have made a remarkable difference

---

Day 294: Offense wins games, defence wins championships #SmartDefence
Day 295: Being defensive promotes blockages, being approachable promotes open doors #BeApproachable

in our beautiful country.

I would like to greet all of you with one saying: your smile is your logo, your personality is your business card, and how you leave others feeling after having an experience with you becomes your trademark.

Lastly, I thank God for giving me the strength and patience during this amazing journey.

Nkosi sikeleli Afrika.

Halala Afrika, Halala!"

The same day, I formulated a Gantt chart (longitudinal plan) on what I would like to do for South Africa and achieve during my reign. Fortunately, I can say that the majority of those plans have been met and conducted. I will talk about these later on.

Perks of being Mr South Africa

A perk of being Mr South Africa is that most of the time, you will get complimentary accommodation from bed and breakfast companies and lodges when approaching them with your title. I have developed wonderful relationships with all of them and till today, spread a word of mouth and exposure for their wonderful hospitality and accommodation.

The other perk was training at Bodytec. This is a form of modern electrical muscle stimulation training that is highly beneficial for one's health, fitness and strength.

With my title, I then established a relationship with Virgin Active where they provided me with a year-long national membership. I also partnered up with Robert Daniels Clothing for them to be my

---

Day 296: *Acknowledge those who have played an integral role in any of your journeys #Acknowledge*

Day 297: *Whatever you do, provide positive implications for society #SocietalImplications*

clothing sponsor. The staff at Robert Daniel have been truly superb and kind, and for that, I will forever be grateful.

I established a wonderful relationship with Ravca Hair Salon to groom my hair. I have never had anyone in my life cut my hair so meticulously and with such accuracy. Carol Naicker, thank you so much for welcoming me with open arms – you have a heart of gold! Janine Reyneke, many have cut my hair, but no one has come close to the perfection, skill and talent that she has. She has greatly assisted in making me look the part for many events.

Events as Mr South Africa

The other perks were being invited to provincial and national events. The turning point for me, was after being invited by Nikki Botha to the Sun Met, when I met one of the most warm-hearted and amazing men, Charl Reineke. If it weren't for him, I wouldn't have attended the other events during the year (Fleur du Cap, Val de Vie, African Odyssey, some theatricals, musicals, comedies and the SA Men's Fashion Show).

Through these events, I met the most amazing people and forged spectacular relationships (both for The Humanitarians and myself). Charl, without a doubt, was my invincible and silent publicist. He never wanted anything in return but just a thank you was enough for him. You don't meet so many like him who have such a warm and huge heart. Independent media have their greatest asset in him.

This is the best part of attending events. Aside from the event itself (in which so much work goes into), you get to eat delicious food, network and meet amazing people, be interviewed by some

Day 298: The man who finishes learning today and stops learning is uneducated the next day #Learning
Day 299: Place more emphasis on skills development with our youth #Skills

television channels and shows (*Top Billing*, *Mela*, SABC News, eNCA, Morning Live, etc) and radio (Cape Talk, Radio702, Heart FM, Radio786, etc). You might even land up in the society newspaper the next day – thanks to Charl!

Criticism while being Mr South Africa

The counter to attending these events is that for me, people would think twice about if I was actually Mr South Africa. I remember fondly the people who had to google it because they didn't believe me (even when wearing my sash). After picking it up on google, they would then approach me and apologise for their ignorance and we would start a conversation.

The sad reality is that there is a major perception in society that a pageant winner or title holder needs to be tall or very masculine with a sexy body. I understand why some may find it hard to believe that I am Mr South Africa 2017. I was even asked if I was part of Mr Teen South Africa due to my height or if I was Mr India South Africa because of my Indian ethnic origin.

I am the shortest Mr South Africa in history, probably the skinniest with less muscle bulk and the first Muslim Mr South Africa. Now being the first Muslim winner, was controversial for many. "How can someone who is Muslim, do modelling and take part in such a competition?" I researched the competition well before entering. If I knew that there would have been implications for alcohol or sex appeal, I wouldn't have even considered it. Mr South Africa was in search for a man of honour and a model-male, not a male model.

The fact that I was a Muslim Mr South Africa was even blown out of proportion. There were those on social media who said some

---

Day 300: *Always be grateful and take note of those who support you genuinely and consistently, these are people you should always keep around #SupportStructures*

Day 301: *The way one treats people is everything. Titles are nothing without integrity and respect #integrity*

bizarre things which obviously didn't affect me: "He is part of ISIS and is going to bomb the whole of South Africa."

Another one: "They chose the Indian because Mr World 2016 is from India." And the best one yet: "First Trump, now Habib, what is happening to the world?"

Lesson: you don't respond or react to such criticism.

You blank it out and pray that God shows them the light. If you respond, they win (in most scenarios). This is what I did with all sorts of criticism and it helped me grow considerably. Some people also see others' success as their failures, which ingrains a sense within them to be bitter and subsequently, be critical or at times, malicious towards others.

One of the things that I also tried to do with my title is to be a role-model to the Muslim youth. I was doing so much for all varied settings but I didn't tap into this setting. I approached a Muslim dominant corporate company and asked if I could use their vehicle to communicate to the Muslim youth on how they can achieve what they set their minds to and how to stick to their morals and values despite the situation. I was informed that their Muslim customer-base is very conservative and would not like the fact that a Mr South Africa had spoken to them.

Curing the mind-set and perceptions of South Africans regarding the Mr South Arica brand, was tough for me, but I tried my best. In trying my best, I had thankfully inspired, served and taught those who believed in me. I had never tried to convince them that I was different. If they didn't believe in me, support me or if I wasn't their favourite, again, I forgave them internally, prayed for them and moved on.

I was also criticised over the fact that everyone thought I had won a BMW. I had saved up for six years and bought my BMW in

Day 302: Wish those all the best in their future endeavours #Endeavours
Day 303: No matter what the achievement or pinnacle, modesty is key #RemainModest

2015 – it was a dream of mine since I was a little boy to drive a BMW; especially after walking to university for those few years. My car was branded as Mr South Africa in order to provide awareness over the fact that I was Mr South Africa, as well as with my personal brand and for our NPO, The Humanitarians. Fortunately, this had provided adequate exposure to The Humanitarians, despite witnessing some eyebrow raising.

Challenges while being Mr South Africa

Because there is no financial gain when winning Mr South Africa (the brand has changed; gone is the day when you would win prestige prizes or money), I had to use my title to accumulate such benefits so that I could leverage better interventions for society.

After I approached some corporates, they told me honestly that they don't want an Indian Mr South Africa and could not unfortunately support me. I responded and said: "While I appreciate your consideration of my proposal and your honesty, I don't appreciate your ignorance." I experienced this on numerous accounts.

Financially, this was the toughest challenge as Mr South Africa. Being in the public limelight and dealing with some criticism was the easiest part, but I also had a full-time job as an academic in sports science.

While my students had embraced and appreciated the fact that their lecturer was a celebrity and Mr South Africa, my work had turned down numerous requests of either giving me time off or lessening my workload. Although I understood the economic climate within higher education institutions around South Africa and the workload that was present at the time, the fact that I was

---

Day 304: Make the most of a platform to inspire and share the importance of living with purpose #UsePlatformsEffectively

Day 305: Feelings are much like waves, we can't stop them from coming but we can choose which ones to surf #Feelings

offered unpaid leave to focus on other areas of my job description using my Mr South Africa title (while reducing my workload) was hurtful and unkind.

I also was cognisant of the fact that the timing of winning the coveted and prestigious title of Mr South Africa during the midst of student protests was not ideal, but it was fortunate in the sense where I got to learn and grow. Specifically, I identified that it was challenging for dynamic individuals to implement change towards teaching and learning, research and community engagement.

If it wasn't for Mr South Africa, I probably wouldn't have come to this realisation and would have spent the remainder of my years at the institution. Don't get me wrong, the years working at the institution were phenomenal, especially from a research perspective. But it felt as if I was hitting a wall and not going anywhere with my energy. I then decided to open the door.

As such, I regrettably tendered my resignation and left in September 2017 so that I could focus more on Mr South Africa. This allowed me to make a further difference to broader societies and communities that are in need in South Africa in my last few months as Mr South Africa. Academia will be there for the rest of my life but the last few months, as Mr South Africa, would not have come again and I wanted to make the most of this opportunity. I knew that this was a sacrifice and investment that would be worthwhile to both my brand and career.

The financial challenge is that I had to raise my own funds for flights, transport, social media posts, photography, etc. One could describe it as a one-man show. In addition to this, I had also received some death threats from the public. They had phoned from unknown and untraceable numbers asking me to either stop being Mr South Africa, to stop what I am doing or to be careful of

---

Day 306: Embrace one of South Africa's favourite activities – braai #Braai
Day 307: New week. New goals. New challenges. Switch off | Switch on #Switch-onSwitch-off

my movements. I was baffled. Why…?

I parked my car at the police station every day and walked to work with someone after also finding out that I was being intermittently followed around. I didn't go to the police for this and open up a case. I didn't want to risk opening this up to investigation, putting it in the public fold and risking having it in the newspapers or on social media the next day.

I needed to protect both my personal brand and the Mr South Africa brand. So I told a select number of friends and made them aware of it. For the first time in a very long time, since 2004 at boarding school, I was scared. I couldn't trust anyone and didn't know who to turn to. I had to suck it up and keep a smile on my face. Yes, Mr South Africa is also human, but I am an ambassador for South Africa and I was carrying the brand of Mr South Africa.

The year 2017 wasn't an easy year for me, but I have grown and I am more than prepared for any other obstacles that may come my way. I am ready for them.

Activities as Mr South Africa

Although the criticisms and challenges have been emotional and exorbitant, the *real* duties and activities were fulfilling, rewarding and enjoyable. Some of the main charity projects / initiatives undertaken during my reign as Mr South Africa:

1. <u>Visits to various hospices and charity organisations</u> (Iris House Children's Hospice, Leliebloem House, CANSA homes around SA, Sarah Fox Children's Home, Universitas Children Oncology Ward, The Friends of the Children's Hospital Association, Red

Cross Memorial Hospital, Kensington Old Age Home and Lily Haven Old Age home).

2. <u>The Sustainable Lifestyle Programme</u> was conducted on the 4th March 2017 in association with The Humanitarians, The Noakes Foundation and Homey Impact in a Community Centre in Mitchell's Plain.

3. <u>Driving for Cancer initiative</u>. I drove 5000km around South Africa (3rd - 19th April 2017) to raise awareness and funding for cancer and the Cancer Association of South Africa (CANSA). R10,000 was raised for CANSA and more than R1,200,000 in awareness value was raised through seven radio stations and five newspapers in addition to educating South Africans. Driving is one of my favourite hobbies and while driving around the country (alone), I got to experience our beautiful country.

Interesting story: when I drove from Durban to Johannesburg, I was on the highway and I think I was driving more than 120 kilometres per hour. The speed limit was 120 kilometres per hour. There were cops on the hill of the road stopping drivers to check their license and if they were driving too fast. The cop stopped me and asked, "Can I see your driver's license please?" I showed it to him.

He then said, "Do you realise you were driving over the speed limit?"

I said, "I am sure I was only about 10 over the speed limit."

He said, "No brother, you were driving 140."

I said, "I would never drive that fast, it's illegal." He then looked at my car which was branded and said, "You are Mr South Africa?"

I said, "Yes officer".

Day 310: *Literacy is the road to human progress and the means through which every man, woman and child can realise his or her full potential – Kofi Annan #Literacy*
Day 311: *Change the face of pageants #ChangetheFaceofPageants*

>He responded, "You must pay more...what kind of an ambassador for our country drives over the speed limit?"
>
>I replied, "Officer, I apologise if I was driving above the speed limit, I didn't think I was driving that fast, but if I was, I am sorry. I am driving to Johannesburg as I am currently raising funds for cancer."
>
>He then said, "Raising funds for charity?"
>
>I replied, "Yes officer, I am now on my way to Gauteng."
>
>He said, "Okay, drive carefully and please don't drive fast."
>
>I agreed respectfully, smiled, thanked him, waved and drove.

4. <u>World Hypertension Day</u> was on the 17th May 2017 and we conducted an educational seminar to teach students from local universities and colleges about hypertension, preventing hypertension and the dangers of sugar.

5. A total of a <u>100 healthy and affordable non-perishable hampers</u> was packed, distributed and educated for an impoverished Muslim community prior to the month of Ramadaan fasting on the 24th May 2017.

6. On the 28th May 2017, I managed to source 20,000 books (fiction and non-fiction; pre-school to tertiary education level). The idea was to mobilise and sustain <u>community libraries</u> among impoverished settings and those that needed literacy. Fortunately, we have distributed a large sum of books to a variety of organisations and schools. The result is that the children are being taught how to read and are improving on their literacy skills.

7. I raised funds for the <u>destitute during winter</u> via BackABuddy. The monies raised, approximately R18,000 was used to keep them warm and give them shelter. In order to make it

---

Day 312: Punctuality is not only about being on time #Punctuality
Day 313: Successful people make decisions based on where they want to be #Decisions
Day 314: Treasure a few quality friends #InternationalFriendshipDay

sustainable we also provided them with sustainable ideas on how they could live off the streets and prevent themselves from being destitute. We also provided a portion of the monies raised to Sedgefield for disaster relief after the terrible fires.

In addition to the above projects and #365heart, I was also invited to be master of ceremonies or speak at various schools, charities and do motivational speaking. No money was made from this. I did this on a voluntary basis. Yes, this challenged me financially, but I couldn't say no to them and had to respect South Africa's economic climate. It was tough for a majority of businesses and organisations.

Aside from community work, what has the Mr South Africa title and platform done for me personally?

Although I did not enter for personal limelight, the best experiences have been appearing on *Top Billing*, *Expresso*, *Mela*, eNCA, SABC News, Morning Live, being featured in a few newspapers and magazines and appearing as a guest on many radio stations around South Africa. I had the privilege of meeting well-known people (Deputy President Cyril Ramaphosa, Archbishop Desmond Tutu, Mmusi Maimane, Jeannie D, Bryan Habana, JP Duminy, and Patricia de Lille to name a few) and being invited as a VIP guest to various events and functions in South Africa.

I also launched my clothing brand using my title as Mr South Africa. Even more exciting will be the launch of Dr South Africa in 2018. I registered this brand so that any person(s) with a doctor's title can use their intellectual capacity to drive change in South Africa. This is something that I will be concentrating on beyond my

Day 315: Contribute awareness towards World Breastfeeding Week #Breastfeeding
Day 316: International Day of the World's Indigenous People #IndigenousPeople
Day 317: Respect women and spread awareness for anti-abuse #WomensDay

reign as Mr South Africa.

What is interesting to note is that Dr Michael Mol (former Mr South Africa - 1996) and I, are the only Mr South Africas with a doctor's title. Now is as good a time as any to provide platforms where there is an emphasis of brawn and heart over beauty. This is the fundamental way of driving change in South Africa and inspiring the youth and people to be better people through skills, education, being healthy, social change and etiquette/values. This is the fundamental message that I also communicated through my TEDx talk in Pretoria: "Breaking Pageant Stereotypes".

Thank you to those who have supported me during my Mr South Africa reign. I have listed all of you in the acknowledgements section. If I have forgotten anyone, I apologise, you know who you are. Particularly, a big thank you to my sponsors, partners and enablers: The Humanitarians, Robert Daniel Clothing, Bodytec, Virgin Active South Africa, The Noakes Foundation, The Residences at Crystal Towers, Spice4Life and Ravca Unisex Hair Salon.

PART 3
THE AORTA

15
LIFE STAMINA

Many people find it challenging to go from one place to the next, from progressing to the next point once they have left the initial point. Through my life journey, I have found out that working hard to get to one point is no easier than working even harder to stay at that point.

So the question is: what makes you go from one point to the next on a consistent basis? The concept that I would like to introduce you to is called *Life Stamina.*

The origin of stamina on its own comes from being out of your comfort zone as highlighted earlier because ultimately we know that this is where the magic happens.

There are a number of principles that govern stamina, about ten in total which can range from: strength, endurance, having a positive mind-set, a prolific temperament, a never say die attitude, perseverance, having a good will power, patience, speed, and consistency.

These ten principles I believe, are the most common and integral aspects that govern stamina.

An analogy that can describe these principles best can be a differentiation between two mountains. I am based in Cape Town and I often hike up Table Mountain, and for those who know what Table Mountain looks like, you will know that it's a steep climb but it is quite flat at the top as opposed to Mount Everest which is the

---

Day 320: *Spread awareness around about African traditional medicine #AfricanTraditionalMedicineDay*
Day 321: *Raise funds and awareness for children with cancer #ChildhoodCancer*

highest point of any mountain in the world.

One would think that it is a lot more difficult to climb up Mount Everest, which of course it is. The difference is that Table Mountain is a steep climb whereas with Mount Everest, most of the distance is a steep walk.

The difference between these mountains is that one requires you to have endurance for distance and the other requires you to have strength and power for climbing. So you need stamina to climb up Table Mountain but you need consistent stamina to climb up Mount Everest.

The question here is: in your life, do you administer endurance through consistency and distance? Or do you administer power and strength over a shorter period of time?

Sport Stamina

There is also something known as sports stamina. When professional athletes run a 100-metre race, the difference between the winner and the person that places last is a difference of split seconds.

Ultimately, when they are training to win a race, they have been training for four years to go the Olympic Games and win a race. The difference between first, second and third place are a matter of split seconds. Therefore, what makes one person have the stamina or upper hand to have a split second advantage over the other? Would you say that is consistent endurance effort or short bouts of power and strength?

At the end of the day, that little bit extra that you put in (as mentioned earlier in the chapter of *Heart*), is what separates you from the other person. There is no limit to the amount of 'extra'

Day 322: Raise awareness and promote the qualities of deaf people #Deaf
Day 323: Improve the awareness on eye care #Eyecare
Day 324: Care for your heart and spread heart health awareness #HeartAwareness

or the 10% that you do on a daily basis. You have to keep on doing as much as you can. Even when running the Comrades marathon, or just marathons in general, thousands of people run marathons but only a select few or less than 30% of them would firstly finish at their desired time, and secondly, only up to 75% will finish the race in its entirety.

The fundamental question here is: do they have stamina to finish the race or to finish within a required time? Or do they have the temperament, the emotional intelligence and the physical stamina to finish a marathon on time?

In the Sports Sciences, when we try to improve the training threshold of someone, we always look at bouts of intensities or levels of effort and these are various increments of about 10%. We start on a low intensity reaching up to a hard and/or maximum intensity.

At each given level, one can improve one's threshold for training by improving one's training efficiency. It is very easy for the majority of people to stop the training routine or consistency and very few would have the life stamina, which amalgamates a combination of consistency, temperament and psychological attributes in order to go to the next threshold and the next and the next. Bruce Lee said it best with his optimal way of describing stamina by always working towards the next threshold: *"If you always put limits on everything you do, physical or anything else, it will spread into your work and into your life. There are no limits, there are only plateaus and you must not stay there, you must go beyond them."*

Day 325: Be proud of your heritage and patriotic values #Heritage
Day 326: Take care of your oral health and promote oral awareness #OralHealth
Day 327: Promote and appreciate the activities of public services #PublicServices

Studying and Academic Stamina

Similarly, with studying, the majority of students study after matric or school. Some take a gap year and then go into studying their Bachelors or some go straight into studying their Bachelors and once they are finished their degree, they take a gap year and then do their Honours studies.

Some don't even continue studying and go straight into work because they want to start making money. But those that go from Bachelors to Honours, after their Honours, some say that they are too tired to study further and feel it's time to make money – they just want to go into the world of work and start making money.

A select few will say, "No we would like to do Masters," or they would like to balance both Masters and work at the same time. After their Masters they get so tired that they tell themselves that they are lacking the research or study stamina to work towards a Doctoral level. Only 1% will go all the way and finish their Doctoral degree (see below figure).

Fortunately for me, in my last ten years at university, I completed my Bachelors, Honours, Masters and Doctoral within a ten-year period without taking any gap years in-between, nor a gap year after matric. This is something that is known as academic stamina.

Stamina means keeping on doing what you can without being interrupted despite what obstacles life throws at you, what your circumstances are, or what challenges you encounter. I was working whilst studying since I came out of matric from my Bachelors right up to my Doctorate through different types of work or different job descriptions; whether it was being a cricket coach, to being a personal trainer, to being a biokineticist and now as an academic and presenter. It has been a long road but a fulfilling one, learning

Day 328: Partake in the 16 Days of Activism against the abuse of women and children #16DaysOfActivism
Day 329: Be grateful towards all sorts of labourers #LabourDay

different lessons along the way.

I look back on this ten-year journey of being at university and I feel glad that I didn't take one year off and I am glad that I have seen through each of these qualifications with consistency and by working smart and having academic stamina. I did not fail any year; I recall that I only failed one module and that one module was during my first year at the University of Johannesburg.

In my second year of university, when I repeated the module, I received a distinction for it because I felt so ashamed after failing it in my first year and I never ever wanted to fail another module at university again. That was the first and only module that I ever failed at university. Thereafter, I learnt an important lesson and carried on my academic stamina, learning from that first important mistake in order to continue until the Doctoral level.

Even for those who work within academia, there is something that is known as the evolution of intellectual freedom. As a student just before grad school, one would say, "I will research whatever I want" but once a student at university, one might say, "I am going to research whatever my professor wants."

The student then graduates and becomes an assistant professor and he/she might say, "I am going to research whatever my tenure committee wants" and then he/she reaches the level of a tenured professor and possibly says, "I will research whatever my grant committee wants."

Eventually, an emeritus professor might say, "I will research whatever" but at this stage he/she has only 10-20 years left of life and that is when the person finally comes to a level of RIP, not 'rest in peace' but 'research in peace'. Throughout that lifespan no one wants to know that his/her evolution of intellectual freedom will eventually come to the grave. Within a space of academia, you

---

Day 330: Do an act of sustainable charity #InternationalDayofCharity
Day 331: Improve the literacy of others #InternationalLiteracyDay
Day 332: Promote awareness on foetal alcohol syndrome #WorldFoetalAlcoholSyndromeDay

want to be a dynamic individual whereby you are enjoying every step, every element of academia, despite what the normal tradition may be and going through different ad hominem procedures.

Despite what ad hominem/promotional procedures you might be working towards; lecturer, senior lecturer, associate professor or even professor, you want to enjoy everything that comes your way. You do not want to make your career such a burden on you that you get to the end, having lost the essence of academia, resulting in you becoming stagnant.

If you become stagnant, it can lead to depression so you want to be a dynamic individual and spice things up for yourself and make it work. In this modern day, many are diversifying their skills. We need to; it is imperative, but of course within the confinements and rules of one's job description or restraint of trade. Although there are many advantages to a career in academia, there are also many associated challenges. The essence of academic stamina is getting through despite the circumstances within academia. You want it to work for you but having mental, physical and emotional intelligence to ultimately maintain stamina within an academic career, is vital.

Work Stamina

Within any form of work, when you reach the end, or retirement at the age of 60-65, this is the start to creativity, it is not the end of the road. A lot of people feel they can't wait to retire so that they can just relax but it is never the end and rather the start of something new. Here again, it is just the mind-set; when you reach the age of 60 or 65, your mind is a predictor of your mental health.

Your mind is the predictor of how far you can go; it is not the

Day 333: Spread awareness and education on gynaecology health #InternationalGynaecologicalAwarenessDay
Day 334: Help and counsel others, and prevent suicide #WorldSuicidePreventionDay

end of the road. That is known in the corporate world as corporate stamina. A lot of people like to climb the corporate ladder in order to reach the top.

They will start off as a junior and try and go as high as possible until they reach the top as either the general manager or even the CEO. But the majority of those in the corporate world only reach the mid-section of that ladder known as an assistant manager or manager and fail to go up to the level of general manager or assistant director or even CEO. The number one reason is that they lack the stamina to keep on climbing and it can take up to about 15-20 years to climb. This is ultimately known as corporate stamina.

There is also something called medical stamina. Surgeons are trained to operate in theatres for hours but they did not receive this training (aside from the theoretical and practical training) during medical school; they received the training during their registrar or specialist training years, which was an ingrained process of the unknown. But from birth they were never trained to perform on a human being or an animal for so many hours and even with being a medical student on call for 24-36 hours, it is not something that you would train for. It is an inherent process that you become accustomed to and not something you learnt about; it's a process you get used to along the years. From this, would you say that medical stamina is born or bred?

Setting Goals to Achieve Life Stamina

Goal setting is fundamental for life stamina. Hypothetically, it is 2018, your plane is currently on the runway, and you want to set yourself a mid-term goal by the end of 2019 and hopefully your plane will start to soar. You have an ultimate goal to achieve something by 2020.

But you can only achieve this goal if the foundation for the years of 2017 and 2018 has been set in place. Remember that the difference between a building and a skyscraper is a solid foundation and if you put that in from now, you will be able to make the difference between a skyscraper and an empire. Therefore, do you have your 2020 vision to achieve your goals by 2020? If you do, you would be able to ask yourself whether you have the stamina to do so. You can even ask yourself: are you the elephant in the room or the lion in the jungle, in order to fulfil your goals by 2020?

Despite the stamina you lead or perform, remember that stamina is not born, but *bred*...

16
LIFE AS A TEST

Johnny's big exam is coming up in two months. He will dedicate most of his time to studying so that he can do well in his exams. For the next two months, he has put all his favourite television programmes, extra-curricular activities and friends on hold. He will devote a bit of his time to them through optimal time-management, but most of his time will be directed at his studying.

His short-term goal is to pass the exams. His mid-term goal is to graduate from high school. His long-term goal is to become a Medical Doctor. As Johnny branches into his journey of achieving goals, he is aware that it will be a challenging yet rewarding journey. Therefore, he will sacrifice whatever it takes to become what he wants to pave a smooth road ahead and most of all, become a doctor.

Along his journey, there are minor and major tests that he might be faced with. He will encounter these tests within his studies and career and some outside of his career (family, friends, community, etc). There will be obstacles thrown at him, a few potholes along the way and some blunt knives where he might find difficulty cutting up some vitamin B. Are his exams the only tests in his life? Or do the rest come as a consequence of where he grew up? For every action, there is a consequence, so has it resulted from what he did?

Johnny eventually pursued his goal of becoming a doctor. He reaped the fruits of his labour and indeed, it was a rewarding

---

Day 339: Provide awareness and raise funds for breast cancer #BreastCancerAwareness
Day 340: Provide awareness and protect marine life #MarineLife
Day 341: Increase awareness on mental health #MentalHealth

experience. He later became a great doctor and was able to provide for his family very well; a comforting home, sports cars, holidays, living the dream. Later on, he was faced with a few challenges and hardships.

He was accused of assault after he was mugged and he had his Doctor's License taken away from him. He was no longer permitted to practice as a doctor. His car got stolen, his home burnt down, his assets were wiped out, and the insurance did not agree to cover the loss. Johnny lost everything.

He was in tears, and felt remorseful and hurt. To him, all of those years of hard work and sacrifice had gone down the drain. He had to start over again, back to square one, back to the drawing board. He thought: *what do I do now? Where to from here? Which road am I taking? What are my wife and children going to do?* Johnny had no parents, as they had passed on after he had graduated, and he was the only child. Johnny went into a depression and ended up having a nervous breakdown.

Later in the year, along his life journey, he came across a man who had witnessed Johnny's struggles and hardships. At that stage Johnny was working as a bartender, yet was still able to give medical advice to customers. They respected him, adored his presence and valued him.

The man was among many other customers whom Johnny had served. As Johnny poured the man a drink, the man had a smirk on his face. Johnny asked: "Am I missing something?"

The man was a philosopher and told Johnny why he had a grin on his face: "You just poured me a drink, and I know the drink will get colder once the ice dissolves."

Similarly in life, we work very hard and wait for the rewards to come and for life to be more 'cooler'. The challenge comes in when

***

Day 342: Provide opportunities and awareness on social development #SocialDevelopment
Day 343: Help someone with transport for a day #Transport

our glass drops onto the floor or gets toppled over. It's not so easy to buy another drink (life), but we can definitely clean up the glass (obstacles) and work towards (pouring) another drink.

Johnny took a step back and thought about what the philosopher had to say and he knew that this glass was him. He might have cracked, but he did not break! The ice is no longer there, but there is potential to make his drink cooler again.

Johnny worked hard as a bartender, saved up for a lawyer, saved up to write his medical exams again, attained his medical degree and started the same road once again. The only thing that was different, was that he was always aware of how something so precious can just slip away from him in an instant. He was therefore careful with future encounters; in life, the social context and with his career.

Johnny was a devoted Christian. He knew it was wrong to steal or to do things which are forbidden in attaining a livelihood. He went through struggle again and reaped the rewards again. From experience, he knows the feeling of working hard for 10 years at something and losing it in an instant.

What do Johnny's experiences tell us? From an exam, to a medical degree, to a collection of losses, he was tested throughout. His exams were not the only tests, but life is a test in itself. If the outcome of passing exams in medical school was becoming a doctor, what would be the outcomes of passing a 'life test'? How do we score it? How do we know if we have passed or failed the 'life test'?

We can all base the outcomes of this test on a variety of factors: religion, culture, ethnicity, moral code or being simple (living in the moment). Some religions see the outcome of the life test as heaven, attaining God's pleasure or fulfilling respective commandments. Following the moral code, people would conduct all actions based on morals and values. Being simple, people would make the most of each day as it comes and live for the moment – something which we should all practice.

Having said the above, there are three ways in which we can classify such tests. Let's use the Chip 'n Dip sizes for example (mini-minor, midi-medium, maxi-major/ultimate).

Mini – passing a school test or scoring a goal in a match

Midi – becoming a doctor or making the national squad team

And Maxi – attaining God's pleasure? Heaven? Fulfilling commandments?

If we view life tests as the above, we can safely say that these tests are in place to develop a momentum to acquiring a maxi (passing the ultimate test – life). We work on the minis and learn skills from these. We progress and excel with the midis and experience a variety of opportunities. We then merge these skills and experiences gathered, so it can become one force to pass the penultimate – the life test.

How we COULD potentially see life or life as a test, is purely up to us. Along the journey, some roads will be smooth, some roads will be bumpy and some will have a detour. Ultimately, it's what we make of it, living for the moment and knowing the bigger picture of life (maxi tests).

Day 346: Keep animals in their natural habitat #WorldHabitatDay
Day 347: Promote the science and knowledge of space #Space
Day 348: Walk to school / walk your kids to school #InternationalWalktoSchoolDay

17

THE ULTIMATUM

Thank you, Mom and Dad

Just when I finished school, my parents separated. I have promised myself since that day and until today, whether they are married or not, I will try my utmost best to be there for them where I can and love them equally.

With that, they also gave me a free reign to do whatever I needed to do after I completed school. Although they barely understood my career path (sports sciences), in which the path that was chosen was less common compared to other careers (medicine, accounting, law, etc.), they gave me unconditional love and support. They also gave me the best gift that any parent could give their child – a free reign and allowing me to strive towards independence.

I am not a parent (I am an uncle and a former cricket coach) but I believe that parents should give a free reign to their children. That will allow them to become independent and better people. However, parents are sometimes cautious of allowing free reign because they are concerned that children or young adults may be attracted to unlikeable distractions or even go astray.

Therefore, discipline and responsibility are key tickets to independence. Only when they display elements of these fundamental attributes, will independence start to become easier for them. Closing them up and restricting the opportunity for them to come

---

Day 349: Promote the study of science for positive implications on peace #InternationalWeekofScienceandPeace
Day 350: Value and appreciate teachers #WorldTeachersDay

out of their shell or get out of their comfort zone, will not assist in both their personal and professional development.

Being over-protective towards your daughters is also understandable. However, empower them to become the best women they can be and support them if they would like to be driven and career-orientated individuals. That is the way modern society is shaping and such women become the driving forces of our country and shape society in becoming a better place. If you allow them that reign, you will be doing society, and your country, a great service.

To all the teenagers and young adults out there, independence will not be freely given on a silver platter; independence is earned. It is something that you will be accountable for in order to earn it; you are the main predictor. If you can practise these core values consistently (not just within your schooling) in all facets of your life, that's when your parents, guardians or guarantors will most likely make the decision to give you the independence and free reign to do whatever you need to do.

With that being said, when that independence starts, it is absolutely critical that you have a good head on your shoulders and have some sense of direction. Otherwise, a direction will take longer to be found, and you will keep trying to take a detour to finding your ultimate dream, career goal or life purpose.

For me, this was the best gift that my parents could have ever given me or my siblings – a free reign to do whatever we needed to do and supporting us to the best of their ability (despite the tough circumstances) or giving us an ear when we needed it.

Thank you Mom and Dad, for allowing me this space from a young age, to chase my dreams and for wanting to do what I had already decided to do, to the best of my ability. This has ultimately shaped the person that I am and has afforded me the vehicle to do

---

Day 351: *Spread awareness and education on bone and joint health #Bones&Joints*
Day 352: *Provide education and support to those with arthritis*
#WorldArthritisDay -World Pneumonia Day - World Sight Day

a lot more by either inspiring or making a difference to the lives of others.

It is an Islamic belief that children are entrusted by God to their parents, to nurture them and raise them as best they can. Children do not belong to their parents but to God. Culturally, our parents take on this pledge rather fervently. With my parents having waited for me for 10 years, hence my name Habib (which means most beloved in Arabic), the intrinsic need to protect me (as well as by my siblings) became unquestioned.

My health scare at the age of seven months (where I underwent an operation because I had suffered from an intussusception – a medical condition in which a part of the intestine folds into the section next to it and becomes tangled), a heart murmur and with asthma, all added further impetus to their protective nature.

Thank you, Khatija and Aslam

My mom kept telling me growing up how my elder siblings, Khatija (13 years my senior) and Aslam (10 years my senior), enjoyed me since I was a baby, whether they played with me on the swings, pushed me in the pram up and down the passage, or gave me some gym exercises after changing my nappy. Being known as the "laatlammetjie", an Afrikaans word meaning literally 'late lamb' – the youngest (by far), till today, they have all given me unconditional love and support.

When I was just two years old, my brother moved to Durban to do his schooling. He used to come home for some of the holidays and I always missed him. Aslam had a massive heart from small. When he came home during the holidays, he would try his best to bring me something from Durban.

I will never forget the set of cars he bought for me – we played with it endlessly! I have no idea how he managed to buy it on a significantly small allowance or at most times, no allowance at all. When he came home, we played cricket in the lounge.

Of course, Mom did not like the idea because it ended up with broken lights or windows. My brother and dad taught me how to play cricket, after also watching cricket continuously. Interestingly, I was very fond of Andrew Hudson growing up. I used to love watching him play and was also glued to his "county" cricket bat.

When I saw that bat, I knew he was batting. When I batted, I used to watch a ball that he faced on television and then face one from my brother. The couches and chairs in the living room were the fielders. If we hit the ball full toss on the chair or couch, it was out. If we broke a window or light bulb, it was out. The fireplace was the wickets.

The passage in the house was 90-degrees to the entrance hall and lounge. I recall using the passage as my run-up and then turning swiftly into the entrance hall to bowl to my brother. My brother had often run away into the kitchen while I was doing my run-up. I ended up bowling to the fireplace realising that he had disappeared. That later used to end up in hide and seek until I relaxed which was either from me getting a slight "eina" (hurt) or being tired.

Cricket in the house later moved to the street. A washing basket or rubbish bin was used for the wickets, and the middle line on the road with the stop street guided us when using the "pitch" and crease.

I think our days of playing cricket on the street stopped after a few years, when I hit the ball on a car passing by which had subsequently broken the window. The result was...my brother and I

Day 356: Educate and provide awareness on spine health #SpineHealth
Day 357: Provide support and care to those with down syndrome #DownSyndrome

running back inside and closing the garage door. My dad later apologised to that gentleman a few days later admitting that we were the ones at fault.

When my brother finished school in Durban, he came back home to study medicine at the University of the Witwatersrand. That was great because it meant that Aslam was coming back home! But by the time he came back, I had moved in with my sister at St Vincent's School for the deaf.

When I went to high school, my brother became increasingly busy with Medical School and he was working extremely hard – either studying, playing soccer or working at the computer labs to earn some part-time cash. After boarding school, I came back home. However, my brother had finished his internship at Baragwaneth Hospital, and he subsequently got a community service post at Themba Hospital in Mpumalanga.

The result was that I barely got to spend any time with my brother since growing up. The times that I got to spend time with him and till now, I make the most of. He is a successful surgeon (after a long and hard road) with a wife and children and this makes it even harder to try and spend time with him when I go visit him. The days we do see each other – is quality time spent together. Both my brother's and sister's happiness means the world to me.

Although my sister was mostly there for me during my childhood years where my brother could not be; the latter years have been different. I have seen more of my brother than of my sister. After my sister moved to Australia in 2003, we have hardly seen her. She has come home now and then but never for too long because she has a family in Australia.

However, I will always know that my sister was there in spirit during my four university graduations and when winning Mr South

---

Day 358: *Provide education, support and care to those with osteoporosis #Osteoporosis*
Day 359: *Provide education and spread awareness on Polio #Polio*

Africa. How on earth can one play such a significant role in a person's early years growing up and then not be able to be there for even one of the person's career milestones? Her heart is so huge to accept that she couldn't be there physically. The skills and lessons that she imparted to me growing up, she now offers to her two beautiful girls, Karima and Zahra. I will always understand why she couldn't attend these milestones. What I am trying to say is that she played such an important part in my developing years so I hope that she will be able to witness at least one of my milestones in the future.

Throughout my life, despite not having spent as much time as I would have liked with my brother and sister, they have always supported me. And I have supported them as best as I can. And during these times, we made the best out of it. I look forward to spending more time with my family and loved ones, and making each day count. Thankfully, technology allows us to keep in touch regularly.

Giving from the heart is the ultimate key to success

As mentioned earlier in the book, giving from the heart was definitely observed and learnt from my family. For me, giving from the heart is the difference between ordinary and extraordinary outcomes. I hope my story has given you that little extra in your life.

I am just an ordinary guy, but became extraordinary through giving from the heart, doing acts of kindness and undertaking all activities from the heart. We all say give 110% in all that you do. I say, do everything from the heart. Because when you do, you also become successful.

Some give their 110% but still wonder why they haven't been

Day 360: Improve the awareness and education on HIV/AIDS #HIV/AIDS
Day 361: Improve the awareness and education on strokes #Stroke

successful? Perhaps it wasn't done with sincerity, devotion and passion. Verily, these are some of the main elements that make daily activities 'heartfelt'. Even if you give 50%, through giving from the heart, you will most likely still come out on top or be very close to achieving your goals.

I am not a fan of diplomacy – it's close to being pretentious or superficial. It is sometimes not real, nor authentic. Professionalism on the other hand, most of the time, is not about being a diplomat. Don't smile because you have to, smile because you want to. Don't do anything because you have to, do it because you want to. Remove yourself from toxic environments and people, as it is not good for the heart. It makes the soul bitter, creating negative thoughts. You can't fix toxicity.

But...your heart is your cleanser and purifier. When it becomes purified, your mind is clearer, fresher and your intentions promote positive actions. Your heart is the fuel to the mind (the engine); leaded, unleaded or diesel fuel. It alleviates the soul and it burns a flame of giving through igniting kindness, which is why it is such a powerful weapon.

We can never be certain of what the future holds but I am certain that my root and the first two branches of life, has provided me with a solid foundation to do more for society. After being crowned as Mr South Africa, I remain humbled and grounded. I can never forget where I came from, the hard yards walked and where I am now.

I look to the future now with a better vision and a mission that I hope will make a difference in the lives of others. If I can contribute towards 5% of difference making in my life, then for me, that would be a significant contribution, and I continue aiming to give from the heart.

Have a heart when living – that's your foundation. Giving from

---

Day 362: Be kind and helpful towards tourists #Tourists
Day 363: Provide education and awareness to those with Diabetes #Diabetes

the heart has been my foundation, and fortunately, the foundation is granite. No one can damage it or take it away from me. It is so strong, that at the age of 29, I look forward to building on it. I pray that God gives me a sufficient number of years in order to inspire and change the lives of millions.

But if I had to leave now, I know that I have planted a heartfelt seed. Or rather, when my leaf eventually falls, I will leave knowing that my root (foundation) was strong because I gave from the heart. I lived, loved and laughed from the heart. Ultimately, I made a difference, which came from a wonderful place, the ultimatum: the heart.

You can do it too...

Day 364: *Promote the rights of persons with disability #DisabilityRights*
Day 365: *Perform an act of kindness and appreciation – finish the year off on a kind note and give from the heart #Kindness&Appreciation*

Acknowledgements

Kooresha Majid (Mom)
Iqbal Noorbhai (Dad)
Dr. Aslam Noorbhai (brother)
Khatija Halabi (sister)
Dr. Abdel Halabi (brother-in-law)
Karima Halabi (niece)
Zahra Halabi (niece)
Zia Noorbhai (niece)
Zara Noorbhai (niece)
Abdur-Rahman Khan
Adam Bulbulia
Adri Winckler
Ahmed Nawab
Albert van Zyl
Altaaf Kazi
Appa Salma Badat
Ayesha Hendricks
Aziz Bhai
Brian Mawdsley
Bruce Lee
Carol Naicker
Charl Reineke
Christo de Ridder

Clive Kirkwood
Coleen Deedat
David Sharp
Dr. Gary Gabriels
Dr. Rowena Naidoo
Faheem Essack
Fatimah Khan
Feizal Kimmie
Gadija Arend
George Banda
Hafiz Pasha Habibi
Hazrat Saeed Soofie
Hazrat Soofie Saheb RA
Heinrich Gabler
Huda Ahmed
Ibrahim Patel
Imraan (Gattuso) Patel
Imran Patel
Jaco Hoffmann
Johann Els
Janine Reyneke
Ken Sharp
Khalil Sayed

Khwaja Habib Ali Shah RA
Lance Walbrugh
Les Lambert
Lindo Phiri
Maliga Naidoo
Marika Sboros
Mariska Brink
Megan Lofthouse
Mehboob Bawa
Melanie Moodley
Melinda Pillay
Michael Harris
Moulana Riaz Seedat
Moulana Sulieman Ravat
Muhsinah Khan
Mukhtar Khan
Mumtaaz Badat
Nabila Noor-Mahomed
Naseema Mustapha
Naseera Noor-Mahomed
Nelson Mandela
Niaz Ahmed
Nikki Botha
Nisaa Goolam Hoosen
Noel Adams
Prof. Tim Noakes
Prof. Leon Lategan
Rafiek Variawa
Rakshendra Pillay
Razeenah Lockhat
Razia Rawoot
Russell Woolmer
Safeeya Mahomed
Salega Tape
Shahnaaz Ahmed
Shameema Hoosain
Spice4Life
Taahira Moola
The Residences at Crystal Towers
Wayne Sparrow
Wikus Otto
Yakeen Sadiq
Zaid Vawda
Zara Kimmie
Zarinah Khan
Zelda Krafft

Glossary

- **Day 1:** #LifePurpose
- **Day 2:** #WorkOfOthers
- **Day 3:** #WomenAndChildren
- **Day 4:** #SharingMeals
- **Day 5:** #MotivationalWord
- **Day 6:** #Diversity
- **Day 7:** #FreshWater
- **Day 8:** #Lead
- **Day 9:** #LoadOff
- **Day 10:** #Talents
- **Day 11:** #SupportHealth
- **Day 12:** #Healthy
- **Day 13:** #Variety
- **Day 14:** #Love
- **Day 15:** #DoMore
- **Day 16:** #Beauty
- **Day 17:** #Calling
- **Day 18:** #HeartfulAct
- **Day 19:** #Confidence
- **Day 20:** #Chivalry
- **Day 21:** #Anti-bullying
- **Day 22:** #Gratitude
- **Day 23:** #Success
- **Day 24:** #VisionAndMission
- **Day 25:** #Animals
- **Day 26:** #CaptureMoments
- **Day 27:** #PeopleBehindScenes
- **Day 28:** #Surroundings
- **Day 29:** #Dream
- **Day 30:** #Hope
- **Day 31:** #NoToxicCharity
- **Day 32:** #Litter
- **Day 33:** #Homeless
- **Day 34:** #Gift
- **Day 35:** #RespectWomen
- **Day 36:** #Exercise
- **Day 37:** #Persevere
- **Day 38:** #Assistance
- **Day 39:** #WorkingBreak
- **Day 40:** #BreakPoverty
- **Day 41:** #YouthSport
- **Day 42:** #GiveAnEar
- **Day 43:** #NoCommunityLimit
- **Day 44:** #ImplementableCharity
- **Day 45:** #MnE
- **Day 46:** #PackAway
- **Day 47:** #Waiters
- **Day 48:** #MeaningOfHumanitarian
- **Day 49:** #Illustration
- **Day 50:** #DeafCommunity
- **Day 51:** #SustainableIdea
- **Day 52:** #ShiftWorker
- **Day 53:** #Knowledge
- **Day 54:** #ProgrammeSupport
- **Day 55:** #CloseUpShop
- **Day 56:** #Message
- **Day 57:** #SignLanguage
- **Day 58:** #Synergy
- **Day 59:** #Support
- **Day 60:** #TheBlind
- **Day 61:** #Surprise
- **Day 62:** #MovieTreat
- **Day 63:** #HardYards
- **Day 64:** #SleepWithTheHomeless
- **Day 65:** #Week-end
- **Day 66:** #FreeConsult
- **Day 67:** #SimpleTeaching
- **Day 68:** #Eid
- **Day 69:** #Student
- **Day 70:** #Shoebox
- **Day 71:** #ParkingSpot
- **Day 72:** #Wisdom
- **Day 73:** #Raffle
- **Day 74:** #CareerMentorship
- **Day 75:** #TimeManagement
- **Day 76:** #InvestInTheYouth

- ❏ **Day 77-80:** #Learn&Teach
- ❏ **Day 81:** #StreetSmart
- ❏ **Day 82:** #Laugh
- ❏ **Day 83:** #FeedAnimals
- ❏ **Day 84:** #KindCompetitor
- ❏ **Day 85:** #Compliment
- ❏ **Day 86:** #NatureConservation
- ❏ **Day 87:** #Hydration
- ❏ **Day 88:** #Presentation
- ❏ **Day 89:** #Seminar
- ❏ **Day 90:** #LiftSomeone
- ❏ **Day 91:** #Approach
- ❏ **Day 92:** #Ice-Cream
- ❏ **Day 93:** #Accessibility
- ❏ **Day 94:** #AcademicMentorship
- ❏ **Day 95:** #Policemen
- ❏ **Day 96:** #ListenToTheElderly
- ❏ **Day 97:** #ShoppingHelp
- ❏ **Day 98:** #SupportYourMentor
- ❏ **Day 99:** #HonestLiving
- ❏ **Day 100:** #OldClothes
- ❏ **Day 101:** #Appreciation
- ❏ **Day 102:** #Ability
- ❏ **Day 103:** #OsgoodSchlatters
- ❏ **Day 104:** #Country
- ❏ **Day 105:** #Youth
- ❏ **Day 106:** #TogetherWeAreStronger
- ❏ **Day 107:** #Soil
- ❏ **Day 108:** #InherentStrengths
- ❏ **Day 109:** #PeacefulMindset
- ❏ **Day 110:** #Hospice
- ❏ **Day 111:** #ConserveNature
- ❏ **Day 112:** #Tolerance
- ❏ **Day 113:** #HumanRights
- ❏ **Day 114:** #Birthday
- ❏ **Day 115:** #Philosophy
- ❏ **Day 116:** #BeKind
- ❏ **Day 117:** #Hospitality
- ❏ **Day 118:** #Prematurity
- ❏ **Day 119:** #Family
- ❏ **Day 120:** #VisionandProcess
- ❏ **Day 121:** #FinanciallyResponsible
- ❏ **Day 122:** #EmbraceChallenges
- ❏ **Day 123:** #KnowYourWorth
- ❏ **Day 124:** #LifeMoment
- ❏ **Day 125:** #wisdom
- ❏ **Day 126:** #OvercomeYourFears
- ❏ **Day 127:** #Water
- ❏ **Day 128:** #Vision
- ❏ **Day 129:** #Perspective
- ❏ **Day 130:** #Health
- ❏ **Day 131:** #PositiveReviews
- ❏ **Day 132:** #SmartWork
- ❏ **Day 133:** #Rooibos
- ❏ **Day 134:** #Ceasefires
- ❏ **Day 135:** #Education
- ❏ **Day 136:** #Heart
- ❏ **Day 137:** #NeverSayDie
- ❏ **Day 138:** #Obesity
- ❏ **Day 139:** #SpecialDay
- ❏ **Day 140:** #LifeCircles
- ❏ **Day 141:** #Criticism
- ❏ **Day 142:** #Principles
- ❏ **Day 143:** #TrueSupport
- ❏ **Day 144:** #Courtesy
- ❏ **Day 145:** #Children
- ❏ **Day 146:** #Listen&Understand
- ❏ **Day 147:** #GreatestAsset
- ❏ **Day 148:** #Blessings
- ❏ **Day 149:** #Leadership
- ❏ **Day 150:** #Doing
- ❏ **Day 151:** #HumanDignity
- ❏ **Day 152:** #Cancer
- ❏ **Day 153:** #LaceUpForCancer
- ❏ **Day 154:** #StepByStep
- ❏ **Day 155:** #Understanding
- ❏ **Day 156:** #Role-Model
- ❏ **Day 157:** #TesticularCancer
- ❏ **Day 158:** #PhysicalDisabilities
- ❏ **Day 159:** #BuildBridges
- ❏ **Day 160:** #WomenScience
- ❏ **Day 161:** #Radio
- ❏ **Day 162:** #UnconditionalLove
- ❏ **Day 163:** #WorldPeace
- ❏ **Day 164:** #SpecialNeedsKids

Glossary

- Day 165: #UpliftYouth
- Day 166: #LifeObstacles
- Day 167: #Success&Failure
- Day 168: #PlanYourRunway
- Day 169: #MotherTongue
- Day 170: #Referrals
- Day 171: #SupportFoundations
- Day 172: #Footprint
- Day 173: #CancerStigma
- Day 174: #SupportFundraisers
- Day 175: #Extraordinary
- Day 176: #LifeStamina
- Day 177: #ChallengeYourself
- Day 178: #Materialism
- Day 179: #JASON
- Day 180: #InspireHealthily
- Day 181: #bonding
- Day 182: #Circumstance
- Day 183: #Humanitarianism
- Day 184: #SustainableTeaching
- Day 185: #TeachTheTeachers
- Day 186: #KidneyHealth
- Day 187: #QualityFriendships
- Day 188: #CountYourBlessings
- Day 189: #Confidence
- Day 190: #Illusion
- Day 191: #ConsumerRights
- Day 192: #StandAndWork
- Day 193: #EducateTheHeart
- Day 194: #RememberLegends
- Day 195: #MandelaDay
- Day 196: #Hardships
- Day 197: #ResponsibleRights
- Day 198: #WasteWater
- Day 199: #Meteorological
- Day 200: #EndTB
- Day 201: #RememberSlavery
- Day 202: #KnowWhatYouWant
- Day 203: #BestVersionOfYourself
- Day 204: #ClosedDoors
- Day 205: #AppreciateYourFreedom
- Day 206: #Collaborate
- Day 207: #ExamMentoring
- Day 208: #PromoteLocal Business
- Day 209: #AutismAwareness
- Day 210: #BuyBreakfast4Someone
- Day 211: #LittleBitOfGoodCounts
- Day 212: #SupportCancer
- Day 213: #Peace&Development
- Day 214: #HealthyImportance
- Day 215: #DifficultRoads
- Day 216: #ConfidenceWithASmile
- Day 217: #MotherEarth
- Day 218: #ScarsTellStories
- Day 219: #ValueYourLife
- Day 220: #Malaria
- Day 221: #ChoosetoShine
- Day 222: #Privileges
- Day 223: #HealthandSafety
- Day 224: #BeABeaconOfHope
- Day 225: #NeverForgetYourRoots
- Day 226: #RespectWorkers
- Day 227: #PressFreedom
- Day 228: #Don'tUnderestimateYourWork
- Day 229: #ActiveGiving
- Day 230: #SupportLocalTalent
- Day 231: #ThinkCritically
- Day 232: #BeCompatriots
- Day 233: #PeopleAreTheTrueAssets
- Day 234: #ThinkBeforeAct
- Day 235: #DedicateAStatus
- Day 236: #BeBold
- Day 237: #AppreciateYourMother
- Day 238: #AppreciateYourFather
- Day 239: #Families
- Day 240: #DRROP
- Day 241: #Hypertension
- Day 242: #TrustInGod
- Day 243: #SupportOtherInspirers
- Day 244: #BeAGentleman
- Day 245: #CulturalDiversityAndDialogue
- Day 246: #BiologicalDiversity
- Day 247: #KeepClimbing
- Day 248: #LiftUp

- ☐ *Day 249:* *#CryingIsNotWeakness*
- ☐ *Day 250:* *#YomKippur*
- ☐ *Day 251:* *#Ramadaan*
- ☐ *Day 252:* *#Fasting*
- ☐ *Day 253:* *#Blankets*
- ☐ *Day 254:* *#PaceYourself*
- ☐ *Day 255:* *#InvolveChildrenCommunityWork*
- ☐ *Day 256:* *#Thankful*
- ☐ *Day 257:* *#LikeMindedIndividuals*
- ☐ *Day 258:* *#Reading*
- ☐ *Day 259:* *#FunforKids*
- ☐ *Day 260:* *#Environment*
- ☐ *Day 261:* *#CelebrateTheSuccessofOthers*
- ☐ *Day 262:* *#Flowers*
- ☐ *Day 263:* *#Ocean*
- ☐ *Day 264:* *#Impromptu*
- ☐ *Day 265:* *#UnderstandMore*
- ☐ *Day 266:* *#HelpTheDestitute*
- ☐ *Day 267:* *#SayNoToChildLabour*
- ☐ *Day 268:* *#ViolenceAgainstWomen*
- ☐ *Day 269:* *#DonateBlood*
- ☐ *Day 270:* *#ElderAbuseAwareness*
- ☐ *Day 271:* *#Goals*
- ☐ *Day 272:* *#LifeCircle*
- ☐ *Day 273:* *#HistoryOfSport*
- ☐ *Day 274:* *#SexualViolenceInConflict*
- ☐ *Day 275:* *#JobRespect*
- ☐ *Day 276:* *#Psoriasis*
- ☐ *Day 277:* *#Yoga*
- ☐ *Day 278:* *#InherentStrengths*
- ☐ *Day 279:* *#Epilepsy*
- ☐ *Day 280:* *#Presence*
- ☐ *Day 281:* *#Pulmonary*
- ☐ *Day 282:* *#shadow*
- ☐ *Day 283:* *#Life&Living*
- ☐ *Day 284:* *#HealthProfessionals*
- ☐ *Day 285:* *#Nurses*
- ☐ *Day 286:* *#HaveAnOpenMind*
- ☐ *Day 287:* *#Authenticity*
- ☐ *Day 288:* *#Balance*
- ☐ *Day 289:* *#Alignment*
- ☐ *Day 290:* *#Inspire*
- ☐ *Day 291:* *#LocalDesigners*
- ☐ *Day 292:* *#CauseAndExpress*
- ☐ *Day 293:* *#Wilderness*
- ☐ *Day 294:* *#SmartDefence*
- ☐ *Day 295:* *#BeApproachable*
- ☐ *Day 296:* *#Acknowledge*
- ☐ *Day 297:* *#SocietalImplications*
- ☐ *Day 298:* *#Learning*
- ☐ *Day 299:* *#Skills*
- ☐ *Day 300:* *#SupportStructures*
- ☐ *Day 301:* *#integrity*
- ☐ *Day 302:* *#Endeavours*
- ☐ *Day 303:* *#RemainModest*
- ☐ *Day 304:* *#UsePlatformsEffectively*
- ☐ *Day 305:* *#Feelings*
- ☐ *Day 306:* *#Braai*
- ☐ *Day 307:* *#Switch-onSwitch-off*
- ☐ *Day 308:* *#Don'tBackBite*
- ☐ *Day 309:* *#Trophies*
- ☐ *Day 310:* *#Literacy*
- ☐ *Day 311:* *#ChangetheFaceofPageants*
- ☐ *Day 312:* *#Punctuality*
- ☐ *Day 313:* *#Decisions*
- ☐ *Day 314:* *#InternationalFriendshipDay*
- ☐ *Day 315:* *#Breastfeeding*
- ☐ *Day 316:* *#IndigenousPeople*
- ☐ *Day 317:* *#WomensDay*
- ☐ *Day 318:* *#InternationalYouthDay*
- ☐ *Day 319:* *#Humanitarian*
- ☐ *Day 320:* *#AfricanTraditionalMedicineDay*
- ☐ *Day 321:* *#ChildhoodCancer*
- ☐ *Day 322:* *#Deaf*
- ☐ *Day 323:* *#Eyecare*
- ☐ *Day 324:* *#HeartAwareness*
- ☐ *Day 325:* *#Heritage*
- ☐ *Day 326:* *#OralHealth*
- ☐ *Day 327:* *#PublicServices*
- ☐ *Day 328:* *#16DaysOfActivism*
- ☐ *Day 329:* *#LabourDay*
- ☐ *Day 330:* *#InternationalDayofCharity*
- ☐ *Day 331:* *#InternationalLiteracyDay*
- ☐ *Day 332:* *#WorldFoetalAlcoholSyndromeDay*

- ❏ **Day 333**: #InternationalGynaecologicalAwarenessDay
- ❏ **Day 334**: #WorldSuicidePreventionDay
- ❏ **Day 335**: #InternationalDayofDemocracy
- ❏ **Day 336**: #InternationalDayofPeace
- ❏ **Day 337**: #WorldAlzheimersDay
- ❏ **Day 338**: #WorldEnvironmentalHealthDay
- ❏ **Day 339**: #BreastCancerAwareness
- ❏ **Day 340**: #MarineLife
- ❏ **Day 341**: #MentalHealth
- ❏ **Day 342**: #SocialDevelopment
- ❏ **Day 343**: #Transport
- ❏ **Day 344**: #NationalInheritedDisordersDay
- ❏ **Day 345**: #InternationalDayforNon-Violence
- ❏ **Day 346**: #WorldHabitatDay
- ❏ **Day 347**: #Space
- ❏ **Day 348**: #InternationalWalktoSchoolDay
- ❏ **Day 349**: #InternationalWeekofScienceandPeace
- ❏ **Day 350**: #WorldTeachersDay
- ❏ **Day 351**: #Bones&Joints
- ❏ **Day 352**: #WorldArthritisDay
- ❏ **Day 353**: #RuralWomen
- ❏ **Day 354**: #WorldFoodDay
- ❏ **Day 355**: #EradicationOfPoverty
- ❏ **Day 356**: #SpineHealth
- ❏ **Day 357**: #DownSyndrome
- ❏ **Day 358**: #Osteoporosis
- ❏ **Day 359**: #Polio
- ❏ **Day 360**: #HIV/AIDS
- ❏ **Day 361**: #Stroke
- ❏ **Day 362**: #Tourists
- ❏ **Day 363**: #Diabetes
- ❏ **Day 364**: #DisabilityRights
- ❏ **Day 365**: #Kindness&Appreciation

www.ingramcontent.com/pod-product-compliance
Lightning Source LLC
Chambersburg PA
CBHW041432300426
44117CB00004B/28